THE NATIONAL TRUST GUIDE

WALL PLANTS & CLIMBERS

❧ THE NATIONAL TRUST GUIDE ❧

WALL PLANTS & CLIMBERS

URSULA BUCHAN

——— SERIES EDITOR ———

PENELOPE HOBHOUSE

BCA

LONDON · NEW YORK · SYDNEY · TORONTO

Published in association with
NATIONAL TRUST ENTERPRISES LTD
36 Queen Anne's Gate
London SW1H 9AS

This edition published 1992 by BCA by arrangement with
PAVILION BOOKS LIMITED
196 Shaftesbury Avenue, London WC2H 8JL

Text © Ursula Buchan 1992
Colour illustrations © Joanna Cameron 1992
Black and white illustrations © Rosemary Watts 1992
Photographic credits listed on page 110

Designed by Elizabeth Ayer

A CIP catalogue record for this book is
available from the British Library

CN 3923

Printed and bound by Printer Portuguesa, Portugal

10 9 8 7 6 5 4 3 2 1

PAGE 2: *Ceanothus arboreus* respond well to training as wall or balustrade plants, as can be seen here at
Bodnant. Note the meticulous use of wires and string.

CONTENTS

FOREWORD

Wall plants and climbers provide an extra physical dimension to the garden. They can be used to extend existing garden colour statements or are themselves design features creating living 'walls' of delight. Stately wisterias and fragrant roses climb on walls or elegant *treillage* to make curtains of leaves and flowers. Twining plants such as clematis clamber over trees, decorate a pergola to give colour and shade, or throw themselves across eaves or roofs. Fine wall shrubs make architectural buttresses against brick or stone walls or are clipped back flat to provide a formal pattern, which is itself beautiful at all times of the year. With their flowers and leaves in season they extend and enrich lower-growing foreground garden scenes.

The walls themselves – or any climbing 'frame' – also give the living plants extra protection from vagaries of the weather, thus allowing experiments with plants just beyond a garden's usual climatic range. In many regions so many beautiful evergreen shrubs and climbers are just too tender to grow as standards in the open but, sheltered by walls of heat-reflecting brick, will survive temporary low winter temperatures and avoid the worst effects of the dessicating 'wind-chill'. Climbing plants and wall shrubs can also be used to disguise less attractive background walls, which are necessarily functional rather than beautiful.

Ursula Buchan writes knowledgeably and inspiringly about the plants which play these 'background' roles. Whilst emphasizing the decorative aspect, showing examples of 'good' National Trust gardening, she never overlooks or minimizes the practical issues. The plants themselves are far from being retiring 'wallflowers'; many that she describes are among the best garden plants available. She distinguishes between the more woody climbers and wall shrubs that give a framework in winter and summer and the many quick-growing seasonal perennials and annuals that rush upwards to clothe a slice of wall or trellis to become the neighbourly companions of more permanent planting. She obviously enjoys the more exotic rarities but stresses the importance of creating a garden frame with reliably hardy old favourites. While giving firm directions for growing and training the plants and preparation of the soil – useful as an *aide-memoire* to the most experienced gardeners and absolutely invaluable to the learner – she never loses sight of the ultimate gardening goal, the creation of beauty. The book, by describing and illustrating many of the plants *in situ* in Trust gardens, gives the reader visual stimulation as well as advice on the practical reality of adapting the grander scale to more modest dimensions of both town and country gardens.

Penelope Hobhouse, Tintinhull, 1991

Rambler roses, such as these at Polesden Lacey, are suited to pergolas, being prone to mildew if grown up walls.

INTRODUCTION

The ability of many, usually fragile, plants to climb to the life-perpetuating light on the backs of sturdier shrubs and trees, is an accident of nature that has had direct and considerable consequences for the design of our gardens.

Imagine how much poorer they would be without climbing plants. Our house and garden walls would be almost bare. There would be little point in pergolas, pillars, arches or arbours. Ugly buildings could not be softened or disguised so easily, nor beautiful ones emphasized. There would be no alternative to walls or hedges for screens. The use of the vertical plane, which adds so much to the success of gardens, particularly small ones, would be restricted to the planting of columnar trees and tall perennials.

This book is concerned with those climbers, their cultivation and their uses, and with that group of wonderful shrubs that do not climb but that are too tender to be grown successfully in the open garden in this country and benefit from having their backs to the wall. (It may seem slightly illogical, but it is a convention when writing about wall plants to restrict oneself to the description of slightly tender woody shrubs, leaving aside half-hardy sub-shrubs, which usually go in front of wall plants and which benefit from the shelter afforded by them. Space, or the lack of it, inclines me to follow this convention.)

LEFT: A successful mix of single- and double-flowered *Clematis viticella* 'Purpurea Plena Elegans' and *C. × jackmanii* at Powis.

RIGHT: Climbing roses thrive growing up the trunks of fruit trees in the orchard at Sissinghurst.

There is almost infinite variety in wall plants. Some need wall-protection to survive the British winter, whereas others simply benefit from it by a more generous flowering and/or fruiting. Some are deciduous, so present a different face according to the season of the year, whereas others are evergreen and can act as a permanent foil or background. Some are woody while others are hardy herbaceous perennials, or tender annuals. Some act as living architectural structures, while others can be used to overlay those structures. Some are simply decorative, while others are fruitful as well. We should employ them to the full, not solely or even mainly for their usefulness and versatility, but for their often-scented beauty, colour, and variety.

I shall try to show the ways in which climbers and wall plants may be used to advantage in the design of a garden, and how an informed choice of the most suitable may be made. In order to help you, there are profiles of twenty of the best (in my opinion) climbing and wall plants widely available, with an abbreviated Checklist for more than 120 others on page 93.

I have included some plants that can grow *in* rather than against walls – so-called crevice plants – but there is nothing about wall fruit. That is not because fruit are unworthy of mention, far from it, but because the subject has already been ably and informatively covered by Francesca Greenoak in her *Fruit and Vegetable Gardens* (also published by Pavilion).

By far the best way of learning about wall climbers and shrubs is to see them growing well in somebody else's garden. Many very agreeable afternoons may be spent in gardens open to the public, such as those run by the National Trust. Although there is little chance of any of us being able to aspire to the quality and variety grown in such wonderful walled gardens as POWIS CASTLE or SISSINGHURST or, unless you live in a very favoured spot, to the range growing at ROWALLANE, MOUNT STEWART, COLETON FISHACRE, OVERBECKS and TRENGWAINTON (to mention just a few that come to mind), there is much that can be learned from these gardens about

the ways of particular plants. This is especially so if you are in the habit of carrying a notebook and camera with you and of assessing, as a matter of course, which aspect a wall faces. This book is no substitute for time spent so pleasantly and fruitfully. However, I hope that the profiles and checklist will act as a useful *aide-memoire*, when you come to choose plants for your own garden.

There will be times, I have no doubt, when you will feel it sufficient just to enjoy the moment, without a desire to possess what you have seen. You may never find a source of *Alangium platanifolium* that you came across at LANHYDROCK, or *Mandevilla laxa* that you fell in love with at COLETON FISHACRE. However, I have tended to concentrate on plants that are reasonably widely available. If you have difficulty, consult *The Plant Finder*, published by The Hardy Plant Society (see page 107).

The variety of ingenious ways in which climbers climb makes for enormous versatility in their use. Roses, for example, have thorns on their stems that enable them, in the wild, to scramble over other shrubs and trees. Jasmines and solanum are scandent, that is, they use their long stems to push through or round other plants. Both types need tying to supports. Many climbers, on the other hand, have the ability to twine round a support, using their leaf stalks (clematis), leaf tendrils (lathyrus) or entire stems (lonicera). These plants can be used to climb over or through other plants and may or may not need help to do so. Then there are the self-clingers, such as those aerial adventitious roots (hedera), or those with sticky pads or hooks on the ends of tendrils (parthenocissus). These need no help, once established.

The growing of climbers and wall plants is, for the keen gardener, a most satisfactory way of spending time outside. It must be said, however, that, with the possible exception of the self-clingers, these plants cannot be put in the ground and promptly forgotten. The gardener is using a natural proclivity, the climbing habit, in the highly artificial environment of the garden and, in the process, giving himself work to do. To perform well, most of these plants need

Camellia japonica, above a stunning white-flowered rhododendron, guard the doorway at Nymans.

regular attention: proper support, pruning, feeding and watering. The work is immensely enjoyable, but it has to be consistent to be successful. Some of these plants are thoroughly fussy as to the conditions in which they will thrive: the requirement for a well-drained but moist, humus-rich soil is not an easy one for the average garden to satisfy. You must also confront your potential weakness for vertigo in order to climb the ladder to put the 'Mermaid' back on the wall. This kind of gardening is not for the cissy, the faint-hearted or the idle. However, I feel sure you are none of these things, and that you will find this the most rewarding gardening imaginable.

UNDERSTANDING YOUR WALL

ABOVE: Walls both shelter and protect tender plants. At
Clevedon Court the slightly tender passion flower,
Passiflora caerulea, thrives.

LEFT: *Magnolia ciliiflora* 'Nigra' (left), *Clematis montana
rubens* (over doorway) and *Schisandra rubriflora* (right)
at Sissinghurst.

WALLS AS SITES

The gardener who possesses walls in the garden is many
times blessed. Walls shelter plants from wind damage, which
not only sears but can even tear the leaves of large-flowered
plants. Walls store the heat of the sun in the daytime and
give it out at night, so tender plants are protected from the
worst cold and are more likely to survive outside, and hardy
plants often flower earlier and better than they would in an
open site because their wood has been well ripened. Many
are also less likely to be affected by spring frosts, which can
burn young flowers and leaves. Walls extend the range of
plants that the gardener can grow, particularly in northern
districts, as can be seen at SIZERGH CASTLE, ACORN BANK in
Cumbria and WALLINGTON, Northumberland; indeed, in parts
of Scotland, the walled garden is the only place where many
generally considered hardy plants will flower well at all. In
wind-swept parts of England, walls can make all the
difference as anyone who has been to GUNBY HALL, eight
miles from the North Sea in Lincolnshire, or BENINGBROUGH
HALL in North Yorkshire, will appreciate. At COLETON
FISHACRE, for example, on the cliffs above the sea in Devon,
the walled rill garden gave protection for tender plants before
the pine shelter belts grew up in the early days of the garden.
At TRENGWAINTON in Cornwall, rare and tender plants which
might suffer even in that mild area, thrive in the walled
garden where once only fruit and vegetables were grown.
The gardener can grow plants like ivies, which, because of
their habit, are as well suited to walls as they are to the trees
they climb in the wild, but also others which would flop
without the support a wall can be made to give. Many wall
shrubs and climbers are scented, and planting them against

house walls means that their fragrance can carry through open windows and doors on summer evenings.

Walls do not quite give the gardener *carte blanche*. Firstly, walls can only work as effective planting sites if some care is taken over both cultivation (initially and in later years) and training, that is pruning and tying. Most shrubs need far more pruning if trained against a wall than ever they do if grown free-standing; they also need sturdy wires and ties, for it is always inconvenient, and sometimes disastrous, for a large, heavy, evergreen shrub to become detached from a wall.

Watering, which may almost be forgotten as far as established shrubs are concerned, never ceases to be an important consideration. This is because most house walls have eaves or gutters, which prevent the rain from falling very close to the wall. This problem is compounded because most walls are made of porous stones or bricks, which absorb moisture almost like sponges. There is often little or no depth of soil close to a house or garden wall, yet the equable wall microclimate will encourage vigorous and thirsty growth.

Those who garden on a shrinkable clay soil, mainly in South-East England, and have shallow house foundations, should avoid large, deep-rooted climbers and wall plants, which might damage house foundations or find their way into drains. I say *might* because the British Standards Institution have published BS5837 on the subject of *'Trees in relation to construction'*, which warns against planting poplars and willows close to buildings on shrinkable clay, but makes only a passing reference to shrubs. Whether you are prepared to take a risk is, of course, up to you but it is wise to be cautious.

There is also the matter of wind turbulence, particularly at the corners of buildings and the top half of solid walls on the prevailing wind side, but also around high walls punctuated by narrow gaps and even in enclosed spaces, such as a courtyard. This is a problem at both CASTLE DROGO and SISSINGHURST, for example. As part of the object of planting many shrubs against walls is to protect them from cold or strong winds, turbulence is plainly undesirable. Even if it does not affect the plants adversely, eddying winds will adversely affect the gardener who must climb a ladder to tie in, or cut back, branches that have been damaged or have come adrift. At CASTLE DROGO self-clinging climbers like hedera and *Parthenocissus henryana* are used to help avoid this problem.

Walls are not suitable for all climbers and tenderish shrubs: their height, or lack of it, to a large extent dictates what may be grown. Low walls are best used for crevice plants, for prostrate plants, or for sturdy shrubs that do not require more than some shelter at the base. It is unwise to plant very tall climbers if the height of the wall cannot match them, unless you intend to add trellis to the top. The eventual size and general vigour of a plant should determine its positioning. It is no use planting a very vigorous climbing rose, which flowers at the end of long canes, against a low wall, for those stems will continually need to be pruned back. The only time this can work is if you plant a rose, say, or a clematis, on a medium-sized shady wall, knowing that they will grow above the wall and turn their faces to the sun. As can be seen in old-established gardens such as NYMANS, some climbers are capable of climbing a long way, given time.

However, the converse is just as bad. Planting a low-growing climbing shrub such as *Euonymus fortunei* 'Silver Queen' against a tall house wall simply accentuates the bareness of the wall. That being the case, it is as well not to restrict your selection solely, or even principally, to slow-growing plants.

Many lists of plants in gardening books give ultimate heights and widths; although always approximate, these should be taken seriously if you do not want climbers that will lift off roof tiles or sway about unsupported above the wall coping. (The Checklist on page 93 gives approximate heights and spreads, where appropriate.)

Many of the difficulties rather gloomily predicted by me may well come together in a hapless town garden. A bed on the shady side of a house, in a narrow alleyway, for example,

An imaginative use of a Japanese quince, chaenomeles, on a balustrade at Bodnant.

is likely to be a dust-dry, sunless wind-tunnel. Although it will look unpromising, however, the owner should not feel defeated. For, as we shall see, there are plants which happily tolerate, even thrive, in such conditions.

Despite the drawbacks outlined, walls are undoubtedly the best sites for growing a wide range of climbing and half-hardy shrubs. They are certainly better than fences that lack their sturdiness and do not, generally speaking, present such an attractive background or foil. Nevertheless, fences do the same job of sheltering plants without needing to be as solid. Open-work fencing, which breaks the power of the wind, without diverting it over the top so that it eddies, can be a better option in a windy position for plants which need shelter rather than heat.

MAXIMIZING ON ASPECT

Practically the most important determining factor when choosing climbers is the aspect of the fence or wall. The best aspect, in the sense of encouraging the growth and flowering of the widest variety of plants, is one facing south or south-west (rather confusingly known as a south-west wall when really it is situated to the north-east) because such a wall receives most of the sunshine available. West walls are shaded in the morning, naturally, and are, therefore, excellent for those plants with spring flowers or tender buds that might suffer damage from the sun warming them up too quickly after an early morning spring frost. The west wall is usually quite suitable for plants that expect a sunny aspect. East walls are tolerated as an aspect by a surprisingly wide range of (hardy) plants, and even north walls have their denizens as anyone who has seen rose 'Madame Grégoire Staechelin', thriving on the north wall at TINTINHULL will testify. After all, many climbers such as honeysuckles, are naturally woodland plants and are happy to have their roots,

Choosing the right plant for the given wall is important. *Clematis montana* is the most vigorous of clematis and so well suited to the tall tower at Sissinghurst.

at least, in shade. Several clematis, for example, do best on a north or east wall, because the colour of their flowers fades in too strong sunshine. The clever gardener can stagger the flowering of a favourite plant by placing one or more specimens of it against walls of different aspect. For example, in the Tower Courtyard at SISSINGHURST, *Clematis* 'Minuet' flowers earlier on the west wall than it does on the north. At BLICKLING HALL in Norfolk, advantage has been taken of the sunken, dry moat facing east to plant *Trachelospermum jasminoides* 'Variegatum' and other tender shrubs. The moat protects then from the cold winds.

There is thus no reason why every wall should not be clothed substantially by a range of climbers.

In the Twenty Top Climbers (page 59) and the Checklist (page 93), the most favoured aspects for each plant are described, but there is not room to take account of the particular conditions that prevail in every garden. For example, the readers may live in a one-storeyed house where a wide range of plants can be grown on a north wall, because the flowers can grow into the light above. On the other hand, he or she may have a west-facing wall at the bottom of the slope in a frost pocket, so that tender plants will be regularly blasted in the spring, notwithstanding the favourable aspect. Walls that face south but that are low and do not provide much wind shelter will not suit *Clianthus puniceus*, say, or *Ceanothus impressus*. Height above sea level also has an effect on the range of plants that can be grown successfully.

Soil has an influence in conjunction with aspect. For example, ivies can do without much light, but if the soil is very moist at the bottom of the north wall (as it sometimes is), they will do less well than if it were dry. Very tender plants, on the other hand, are more likely to survive winters if the soil is on the dry side, generally speaking.

I hope it will be cheering to read the Checklist and discover just how many plants actively enjoy a semi-shaded or shaded position. There are, after all, shrubs such as *Berberidopsis corallina* and *Camellia* 'Donation', that are as beautiful as most plants that need sun.

WALL PLANTS

1   *Clematis armandii*
2   *Chimonanthus praecox*
3   *Akebia quinata*
4   *Chaenomeles specicosa 'Simonii'*
5   *Abutilon × suntense*
6   *Carpenteria californica*
7   *Wisteria sinensis*
8   *Cistus ladanifer*
9   *Cobaea scandens*

WALL PLANTS

10 *Piptanthus nepalensis*
11 *Ceanothus impressus*
12 *Fremontodendron* 'California Glory'
13 *Solanum crispum* 'Glasnevin'
14 *Buddleja crispa*
15 *Abelia × grandiflora*
16 *Ceanothus* 'Autumnal Blue'
17 *Clematis* 'Niobe'
18 *Abeliophyllum distichum*

The massive stones of this wall provide a good background for delicate flowers, such as *Clematis paniculata*.

THE RIGHT SORT OF BACKGROUND

Until now, we have been discussing walls and fences as if they already existed in the garden. However, there are, of course, occasions when we may have to gird up our loins and build or, more likely, commission someone else to build permanent structures. What these are will mainly depend on cost and inclination, but it is as well not to forget entirely the requirements of the plants that will, it is hoped, find their way up these structures.

I have no space to discuss the business of building, applying for planning permission and so on. My concern is with the aesthetic appearance of garden walls, fences and so on as a background to plants. It will be the counsel of perfection, of course, for this is a matter on which cost and the difficulties of finding materials often lead to compromise.

If you live in a stone-rich area, you will wish, no doubt, to build in stone, for nothing fosters a sense of place better than the use of local materials. However, if this is not available or affordable, reconstituted stone that 'matches' is a possibility. Bear in mind however, that although this comes in different sizes, they are uniform different sizes. They can also look excessively rubbly. Be prepared, therefore, to clothe them extensively with climbers. An alternative is a good quality brick that is similar in colour to the local stone.

Natural stone, being relatively uneven in shape, can be built either with or without mortar. Both 'dry' and 'wet' walls look well as a background. Whichever is chosen, it is an advantage to put in the masonry nails or straining bolts at the time of construction, if possible, for they are hard to put in afterwards, even into a 'dry' wall.

We must not forget the wall itself. Some plants, particularly the self-clingers that support themselves by aerial roots or sticky pads, can harm old walls that are kept together by lime mortar. This is not a reason for banning them outright, simply for being vigilant.

Take note of a word of caution. Miss Gertrude Jekyll, a great lover of climbing plants, entitled one of the chapters in *Wall and Water Gardens*, 'When to let well alone'. It is

A carefully framed view: the rose is trained to emphasize the circular nature of the portal, echoing the
armillary sphere beyond.

The angles of this famous brick wall at Chartwell are softened and the redness muted by the use of climbers, in particular the very Kentish plant *Humulus lupulus*.

PAGES 22 AND 23: The distinctive architecture of the wall to one side of the parterre at Erddig is enhanced by the consistent but restrained use of climbing plants.

tempting when there are so many beautiful climbers to clothe every square inch of wall space with them. However, there are some walls that, because of fine or distinct architectural features, are better off without a smothering of vegetation.

Those who visit National Trust gardens will know how stunning some of their garden walls are. Often made of hand-made brick and mellow with age, they represent the perfect foil for the majority of climbing plants. It is possible to go some way towards emulating this, even if you cannot add the patina of years, by tracking down second-hand bricks or new handmade bricks. Both will be expensive, however. If prohibitively so, try to choose a modern facing or engineering brick that is frost-resistant and does not have too glaring a face. If you use facing bricks, the wall must have a coping on the top. Both for brick and stone walls, avoid coloured mortars unless you wish your wall to date very obviously from the latter half of the twentieth century.

Far and away the worst option, aesthetically, is the screen block concrete wall, which will give your garden an *ersatz* Mediterranean atmosphere. It has to be said, however, that these blocks are relatively cheap and climbing plants of the twining or scandent persuasion will soon soften the edges, without much help from you.

Fences are a cheaper option than most kinds of wall and can look perfectly pleasant, especially the openwork type of trellis. They are usually made from softwood and will have to be treated with a plant-friendly preservative before you erect them. You must also put the posts in metal 'shoes' or concrete bases so that they do not rot in the ground and stretch wires between the wooden uprights. Much fencing, particularly the panel sort, comes ready-made in sections, and consists of either horizontal or vertical slats that overlap. This means that the fence suffers from the same limitation as

Actinidia kolomikta is set off well by the fine old wall, such as are enviably common in gardens run by the National Trust.

a solid wall as far as wind eddying is concerned. Openwork fencing, on the other hand, avoids buffeting and allows your climbers a toehold without the need for much tying in, but it is not very suitable for those climbers, like roses, that need regular pruning. At TINTINHULL, however, a sturdy variety of trellis is used freestanding as a support for a very vigorous rose, 'Bobbie James'. Very thin trelliswork is ideal if nailed on battens and fixed against an ugly wall; alternatively expandable PVC trellis, in white, brown or green, can be used if you are desperate. Other types of fencing include plastic-coated chain-link fencing, which is not attractive, but is a boon for lonicera, sweet peas and other twiners to climb.

I have to say that, as in so many aspects of life, you get what you pay for. If you are prepared to spend a little money, you will not only achieve an effect that is handsome in itself (and thus an enduring pleasure), but that also serves as a good background and support for wall plants and climbers.

WALL PLANTS: STYLE AND FUNCTION

As a conscientious gardener, you will need to make a list of which climbers and wall shrubs will grow on your wall aspects and in the soil that you have, taking into account the severity or otherwise of winters in your district. Try to make a realistic assessment of what will thrive, rather than merely survive in your garden. Once a shortlist of suitable plants has been drawn up, you can move on to the more sophisticated and infinitely more enjoyable pursuit of choosing your plants to make a harmonious design.

Even the basic principle of design that dictates that wall plants suit particular types of building is sometimes ignored. For example, not everyone is careful to avoid putting *Parthenocissus quinquefolia* against a modern red brick house wall. Then, when the leaves turn to their brilliant hue in autumn, they will clash violently with the brick of the house.

The plant's natural habit also matters: a spindly late-flowering clematis such as 'Hagley Hybrid' looks mingy when trained up a substantial wall, but thin crossbars on a pergola can easily look overburdened, even if they are not actually structurally damaged, by a rampageous rose such as *Rosa filipes* 'Kiftsgate'. If the architecture of the house is massive, then large shrubs with big leaves should be planted against them. The two fine *Magnolia grandiflora* outside the house at KILLERTON, for example, fit their surroundings very well. At CHIRK CASTLE, the self-clinging and vigorous *Hydrangea anomala petiolaris* plays host to more frail-looking honeysuckle and roses on the castle wall. By contrast, delicate-stemmed clematis can be left to climb through more substantial wall shrubs or climbers, or kept for clambering up thin posts or trellis.

LEFT: The leaf colours of this Boston ivy, *Parthenocissus tricuspidata*, are brought out fully by the neutral grey wall up which it is scrambling.

RIGHT: A detail of the South Cottage at Sissinghurst, showing rose 'Madame Alfred Carrière' and *Fremontodendron* 'Californian Glory'.

Wall plants should enhance buildings without obscuring important architectural features, as seen at Killerton where two stately *Magnolia grandiflora* flank the front door.

PLANTS IN HARMONY

As important as suiting plants to the architecture, is suiting plants to each other. It is a curious fact that, however careful gardeners are over the design of their borders, they seem to lose all sense of design when they come to consider wall plants. If it will grow there, plant it, regardless of its neighbours or the constraints imposed by architecture – or so the thinking goes. Most gardeners are so glad that they have found something to grow on a north wall, or so keen to cram as many plants as possible in a favoured spot, that they put rose 'Masquerade' next to 'Handel' and yellow-leaved ivies with pink clematis. One can understand exactly how it happens. Apart from anything else, few gardeners have a blank canvas on which to paint their garden pictures, and there is an understandable reluctance to rip out, say, a large, established rose, climbing to the eaves, because it does not really 'go' with anything else.

Nevertheless, good harmonies are possible. At POLESDEN LACEY, for example, the deep red pendant flowers of *Ribes speciosum* harmonize well with the blue *Ceanothus impressus* on the south-facing wall behind the herbaceous border. Harmony is also achieved in the same garden by the restrained use of rambler roses on the long cruciform pergola in the Rose Garden; it is entirely planted with nine varieties, in white, pink and red: 'Dorothy Perkins', 'New Dawn', 'Hiawatha', 'Excelsa', 'Sanders' White Rambler', 'Crimson Shower', 'Minnehaha', 'Albertine', and 'American Pillar'.

At SISSINGHURST, the red flowers of *Clematis* 'Madame Edouard André' set off the pink ones of *Viburnum* 'Pink Beauty', through which it is climbing in the Rose Garden; in the same garden, the deep pink *Clematis* 'Étoile Rose' associates well with the similar *Indigofera heterantha*.

In the Walled Garden at PENRHYN CASTLE, there is a striking group of climbers, flowering in May and June, consisting of the purple-mauve and yellow *Solanum crispum* 'Glasnevin', the butter-yellow *Fremontodendron* 'California Glory', and the purple-leaved *Vitis vinifera* 'Purpurea'. In the same garden, the very vigorous *Clematis montana* is trained all the way

Clematis 'Perle d'Azur' form a particularly successful colour scheme at Sissinghurst.

along and over a 1.2 metre high retaining wall that stretches between two flights of steps. Because of its purplish leaves, it looks particularly good as an understorey for *Nepeta* 'Six Hills Giant' and a yellow potentilla that are growing above it on the top terrace.

If your courage fails you, gentle but pleasing harmonies can be wrought using different cultivars of the same genus. The forms of *Clematis macropetala* 'Markham's Pink' and 'Maidwell Hall', would blend well with the straight species and you could guarantee they would flower at the same time. One of the best known and most successful examples of blending similar plants is the Purple Border at SISSINGHURST, where purple, mauve and deep red large-flowered clematis line the south-facing wall, exploding into a burst of deep and satisfying colours in July.

OVERLEAF: The best walled garden of all. Note the unusual semi-circular wall in the Rose Garden at Sissinghurst.

A simple but startling contrast achieved at Tintinhull using *Clematis* 'Étoile Violette' and the common honeysuckle.

Clematis 'Étoile Violette', *Vitis vinifera* 'Purpurea' and *Rosa glauca* create a harmonious flower and foliage effect.

There are instances when, for a change, contrasts rather than harmonies work well: the orange *Campsis radicans* with *Solanum crispum* 'Glasnevin', for example, or, at POLESDEN LACEY, rose 'Mermaid' intertwined with the pale purple *Clematis* 'Victoria' on the west-facing wall of the Rose Garden. At TINTINHULL, there is a very effective colour combination on the garden loggia, consisting of *Vitis vinifera* 'Purpurea', with orange *Eccremocarpus scaber* and the deep purple *Clematis* 'Jackmanii Superba'.

Flowering at the same time is not always quite enough, for it can leave an even larger gap when both go out of flower. It is necessary in places to ensure a succession. At PENRHYN, for example, the winter-flowering *Jasminum nudiflorum* is followed in spring by *Akebia quinata*, growing through it. Here there is an intriguing contrast, not of flower but of foliage.

When considering harmonious or contrasting relationships, do not forget the impact of foliage, particularly as flowers are so often short-lived. It is more satisfying to see a mixture of deciduous and evergreen climbers than all one or the other, although there are some occasions when the use of just one plant works well: an example of this is the red brick east-facing garden wall at POLESDEN LACEY, which is almost completely covered in *Hedera colchica* 'Dentata'.

Another possibility is to plant *Vitis vinifera* 'Purpurea', next to *Clematis tangutica* 'Bill Mackenzie', which has yellow 'orange-peel' flowers that turn to silver seedheads at the same time as the vine turns deep red in autumn. The vine is such a versatile foliage plant, for its young leaves and tendrils are grey-white and act, with the purple larger leaves, as an excellent foil to the blue-mauve *Clematis* 'Perle d'Azur' on the semi-circular wall in the Rose Garden at SISSINGHURST.

The variegated leaves of *Actinidia kolomikta* make a successful background for any pink rose such as 'New Dawn', a blue-flowered ceanothus, or the silvery-grey leaves of *Buddleja fallowiana*. *Ampelopsis brevipedunculata* 'Elegans' would also be a good bet with the buddleja. Any ceanothus, particularly a deep blue one like 'Cascade', will look handsome behind the yellow pea flowers of *Coronilla glauca*.

A fiery fruit, flower and foliage combination might be achieved by using *Vitis coignetiae*, *Pyracantha coccinea* 'Lalandei', and *Fuchsia magellanica*; or a more downbeat partnership could be forged between the green-yellow fruits of chaenomeles and the flowers of *Clematis* 'Alba Luxurians'. Nor must it be forgotten, although out of the scope of this book, how the impact of many wall plants can be enhanced by the perennials growing in front of them in the border.

CAMOUFLAGE CLIMBERS

To some gardeners, or at least garden owners, climbing plants are synonymous with those that cover, rather than those that merely highlight, architectural features. Certainly the disguising, or masking, of car ports and other unlovely outhouses is a very useful function of climbers. Best-known of the plants to do the latter is the Russian vine, *Fallopia baldschuanica*, the so-called 'Mile-a-Minute Plant', but it can cause real problems to gardeners because it is so vigorous. For the same reason, strong-growing roses such as *Rosa filipes* 'Kiftsgate' are rarely a good idea. If you doubt the solidity of the structure, and the site is sheltered, choose something moderately lightweight and evergreen, such as *Clematis armandii* or *Hedera colchica* 'Dentata'. If the position is not very favourable, *Holboellia coriacea* is hardy and will grow in shade. Avoid deciduous, annual or herbaceous climbers that, although otherwise suitable, have the disadvantage of shedding their leaves, thereby both blocking gutters and leaving the building stark in winter.

Unfortunately, the list of suitable plants is limited by the fact that many evergreen climbers are not very hardy, and need a sheltered spot to thrive. It may be necessary to grow an evergreen against, rather than over, the roof, and for this the ivies are useful for a shaded place. On the long north-facing garden wall at ERDDIG, an extensive and instructive collection of ivies has been planted in deep shade. Here can be found *Hedera helix* 'Atropurpurea', which is a vigorous ivy with purple leaves in winter, which will grow 4m / 13ft tall, as well as *H.h.* 'Ivalace', which has dark green

Parthenocissus quinquefolia is a suitable plant for camouflage; it provides interesting leaf-shape and colour.

Another effective camouflager is the ivy *Hedera colchica* 'Dentata Variegata', seen here at Beningbrough.

curled leaves and scarcely reaches one metre. *Garrya elliptica* will grow in sun or shade, and can do a good job of covering up, because the leaves are comparatively big and evergreen. It makes a dense shrub growing up to about 4m / 13ft in time. *Camellia × williamsii* 'J.C. Williams' is another excellent plant, provided the soil is not limey, because it has pleasing arching stems, a broad habit and drops its pretty pink flowers once they have faded.

If a deciduous climber is required, then a reasonably vigorous species of clematis, such as the spring-flowering *Clematis macropetala* or the autumn-flowering lemon-coloured *C. tangutica*, is also suitable. The second has woolly seedheads lasting into winter and will grow on any aspect, although it does not like cold winds. An unusual and very vigorous climber is the deciduous *Celastrus orbiculatus*, which likes a shaded position and will grow up to about 12m / 40ft. It has black fruits that open to reveal striking scarlet seeds at the same time as the leaves turn yellow. Finally, there are, of course, the invaluable self-clingers, *Hydrangea anomala petiolaris* and *Schizophragma integrifolium*, whose only fault is a slight reluctance to get going initially.

There are times when it is not necessary to hide a building, merely advantageous to screen it; to make it less obvious, or more interesting, or simply to soften its sharp rectilinear lines. Well known for achieving all of these is the Virginia creeper, *Parthenocissus quinquefolia*, which shows what it can do on the massive neo-Norman castle walls at PENRHYN. Also very suitable for this aesthetic purpose are the pyracanthas, which can be trimmed in early summer; they will lose some, though by no means all, of the flowers (and therefore fruit) if treated in this way.

The neo-Norman castle of Penrhyn, looking towards Snowdon, with a covering of Virginia creeper, used not to hide the massiveness of the castle walls but to soften their starkness.

Low walls can be screened from above with a prostrate evergreen plant such as *Ceanothus thyrsiflorus* 'Repens', which can be trimmed after flowering in June, or *Rosmarinus × lavandulaceus* (syn. *R. officinalis prostratus*) as used at TRERICE, or even *Cotoneaster horizontalis*. The most beguiling effect is created at GUNBY HALL by *Rosa* 'Paulii' which hangs down the brick side of the Ghost Walk pond, its great white star flowers almost touching the water.

At BODNANT, imaginative use is made of the many, wide (0.75m / 2½ft) balustrades that flank the steps between the south-facing terraces. Here plants, such as roses, clematis, and wisteria, are tied up and along galvanized wires stretched on the top. The same thing is done on the garden terrace at UPTON with two vigorous roses, 'Albertine' and 'Leverkusen'. The idea is plainly not to hide what is fine stonework, but to soften, even accentuate it. Without those climbers, the visitors would, paradoxically, be less conscious of the balustrades. Similarly at NYMANS very vigorous climbers, such as *Rosa banksiae* 'Lutea', grow on the part of the old house devastated by fire, and serve to underline the starkness of the glassless, mullioned windows and ragged stonework.

Of course, at BODNANT, both the fine stone steps and the balustrade almost disappear under the leafage of *Wisteria venusta* and *W. floribunda* 'Alba', on both sides of the fountain on the Croquet Terrace. The effect is too spectacular in May and June to justify any grumble about the disappearance of the stone.

LEFT: The façade of the Orangery at Powis Castle boasts a mixture of wall plants including wisteria, *Abutilon vitifolium album* and *Magnolia grandiflora*.

RIGHT: At Nymans, very vigorous climbers, such as *Rosa banksiae* 'Lutea', find a hold among the glassless, mullioned windows and ragged stonework of the ruined house.

ARCHITECTURAL CLIMBERS

You can also use plants with enough bulk or leaf to help divide an open space. This is a highly respectable tool of garden design that is not used as much as it might be. By the use of trellis, attached to wooden or brick pillars, for example, it is possible to create a barrier that is reasonably cheap in comparison to a solid architectural structure like a wall, less dense and quicker growing than a hedge, and that will change with the seasons. It will also give tantalizing glimpses of what there is beyond, a particularly helpful device in small gardens. If hardy climbing plants are used in this way, they can also perform the practical function of shielding more tender plants, which are planted below.

The best climbers for trellis or openwork fences are those with twining stems or leaf-stalks, which require little or no pruning attention, such as the yellow-leaved *Humulus lupulus aureus* (which is a hardy herbaceous perennial), the honeysuckles, *Jasminum officinale*, species of clematis and the evergreen *Hedera canariensis* 'Gloire de Marengo'. Hardy evergreen shrubs that benefit from a little support, such as *Ceanothus* 'Autumnal Blue', would also be suited to such a situation. The annual climbers are particularly suited because they leave the fence or trellis free in winter, allowing you to treat it with preservatives.

It may be that a more solid living barrier is required, say, to break up a long wall border into sections. This can be done informally with a large wall shrub that reaches from back to front, even spilling over the path if the impression of profusion is required. An example of this is a very large specimen of the evergreen *Viburnum tinus* in the south-facing border at HARDWICK HALL. Other wide-spreading shrubs suitable for this purpose in a sheltered spot, are the escallonias and *Crinodendron hookerianum*. The yew 'tumps' at POWIS serve the same purpose aesthetically and practically, providing shelter and even some necessary shade for wall plants on the terrace below.

Alternatively, small-leaved evergreens, the kind suitable for hedging, can be planted to make trimmable buttresses. A

In a shady corner the evergreen shrub, *Taxus baccata* 'Fastigiata', not usually known as a wall shrub, has been used to break up the monotony of the wall.

tenderish plant like *Pittosporum tenuifolium* (or one of its coloured-leaved varieties like 'Purpureum', 'Variegatum' or 'Silver Queen'), all of which like to feel a wall at their backs, will perform this function admirably, in a sheltered warm border at least. The hardy yew can be used in the same way. At OXBURGH, bay trees (*Laurus nobilis*) are grown on the west walls to help break up a very long wall. Not only can they be used as cheap architectural features, but they can act as additional shelter for tender plants, or even tender people working in the border. This is one of the easiest ways of creating a favourable microclimate.

RIGHT: A view of the famous yew 'tumps' at Powis which are echoed in the foreground by 'Jackman hoops', hidden under the mass of clematis which they support.

RAPID GROWERS

It is all too tempting, particularly in a new garden, to settle for rapid growers to screen walls, or add height in a hurry. There are several commercially-available types, but do use them with discernment, for, though they can get you out of a jam, they are just as likely to land you in the soup. Climbers, as a class, usually grow fast – in comparison with the normal run of shrubs, at least. The ability to climb at all is a response to dark conditions in a woodland setting, and the faster it can be achieved, the better likelihood of survival. Those that excel themselves in this regard should be treated with caution. *Fallopia baldschuanica*, mentioned above, for example, should not be planted anywhere in the flower garden, although I do like to see it in a semi-wild place for the pleasure of its myriad white flowers in July, which turn pink as they fade.

Also very fast-growing, once established, are the climbers *Vitis coignetiae, Parthenocissus quinquefolia, Campsis radicans, Aristolochia durior, Solanum crispum* 'Glasnevin', the jasmines, most clematis such as *C. flammula,* and vigorous roses like 'Bobbie James' and *Rosa longicuspis.* Among the shrubs, I have found *Abutilon × suntense* grows rapidly, provided it is given a warm sheltered place, as do the ceanothus family, buddlejas, and *Forsythia suspensa.*

Not surprisingly, there are some excellent rapid growers amongst the annual climbers, and these are enormously useful – provided, that is, they are not expected to act as permanent screening plants, for they are usually cut down by the first frosts. They are, in fact, often perennial but too tender to survive one of our winters, so are treated as annuals. One of the best known is *Eccremocarpus scaber,* the climber with grey-green leaves, thin orange trumpet flowers and bladder seed pods. This plant will survive a mild winter in a sheltered place. *Cobaea scandens,* the cup and saucer plant, of which there are both blue-mauve and white forms, is another very handy fast grower. Another, becoming more popular of late, is *Rhodochiton atrosanguineus,* a strange plant from Mexico, which has pendulous red-purple flowers with a protruding darker corolla from August until October. Better known, but just as garden-worthy, are the morning glories, most particularly *Ipomoea tricolor* 'Heavenly Blue', and also the yellow-flowered *Tropaeolum peregrinum.* At KILLERTON, for example, *Tropaeolum peregrinum* climbs up through *Magnolia grandiflora* on a house wall. The attraction of these plants lies not only in their desire to reach for the sky, but also the variety of exotic flowers they bring to our summer gardens.

PERFUMED WALLS AND FRUITY BOWERS

We should not forget how large is the proportion of climbing and tender wall shrubs that have scented flowers or leaves, or both, which makes them worth almost any amount of effort. To mention just some of the better known: *Abelia grandiflora, Abeliophyllum distichum, Akebia quinata, Azara microphylla, Buddleja crispa, Carpenteria californica, Ceanothus* 'Gloire de Versailles', *Chaenomeles* (fruit), *Chimonanthus praecox, Choisya ternata, Clematis armandii* 'Snowdrift', *Clematis flammula, Coronilla glauca, Cytisus battandieri, Dendromecon rigida, Drimys winteri, Jasminum humile* 'Revolutum', *Jasminum officinale, Jasminum × stephanense, Lathyrus odoratus,* most lonicera, *Magnolia grandiflora, Myrtus communis,* many roses, *Schisandra rubriflora, Solanum crispum* 'Glasnevin', *Trachelospermum jasminoides, Wisteria floribunda* and *W. sinensis.* It is impossible in public gardens always to gain the full benefit of scent, not only because standing in flower borders is not encouraged, but also because many scented plants exhale their strongest breath on warm evenings, when the gates have long closed. However, at TRELISSICK, there is a small walled garden, specially planted with aromatic plants, which is worth a visit at any time of the summer.

Although it is tempting to concentrate exclusively on those plants that, from the design point of view, are beautiful or useful, we should not forget that many plants are trained against walls in order to encourage their fruitfulness. Fruit trees may well avoid damage from late spring frosts if planted against walls, and will usually benefit from the additional warmth and shelter by fruiting better or more

A fruitful and aesthetically pleasing combination of wall-trained pears and plums, growing among spring-flowering polyanthus.

prolifically. There is an aesthetic function too: wall fruits, trained in restricted forms (espaliers, cordons or fans) look very pleasing, as anyone who has been to FELBRIGG HALL, WESTBURY COURT, STANDEN or ERDDIG will know.

PLANTS FOR TRICKY SPOTS

There are times, unfortunately, when aesthetic considerations must take second place to practical ones, however. Most gardeners have an area of garden (or perhaps the whole garden) that they would describe as unpromising or difficult. Of course, one man's poor, dry, baked soil is another man's ideal spot for *Abutilon × suntense*, but there is some consensus on problem places: shady or frost-prone walls, heavy clay soils, extreme acid or alkaline soils, and cold exposed positions. This is when the gardener reaches for the list of obliging plants. Fortunately, there are, amongst climbers particularly, some very amenable plants which would be worth growing in any event.

On a north wall at POLESDEN LACEY, for example, may be found *Rosa* 'Madame Sancy de Parabère', 'Maigold', 'May Queen', 'Madame Lauriol de Barny', *Clematis flammula*, *Jasminum nudiflorum* and *Hedera colchica* 'Sulphur Heart'. With the exception of the ivy, *Clematis flammula* and possibly *Jasminum nudiflorum*, one would not normally expect to see those plants on a north wall. In National Trust gardens some, usually justified, risks are taken.

More generally recognized as suitable shrubs for a north wall are: *Azara microphylla*, *Camellia japonica* and *C. × williamsii*, most chaenomeles, *Crinodendron hookerianum* (if the soil is acid), *Desfontainea spinosa*, *Eucryphia × nymansensis*, *Euonymus fortunei*, *Garrya elliptica*, *Jasminum nudiflorum*, *Kerria japonica* 'Pleniflora', *Mahonia japonica*, *Piptanthus nepalensis*, and pyracantha; climbers include *Akebia quinata*, *Celastrus orbiculatus*, *Hedera colchica* and *H. helix*, *Hydrangea anomala petiolaris*, muehlenbeckia, parthenocissus, *Schizophragma hydrangeoides* and *S. integrifolium*.

Heavy clay soils are inimical to many tender wall plants, particularly the evergreens, but there are some that are more tolerant, such as chaenomeles, cotoneaster, forsythia, lonicera, mahonia, pyracantha and most roses.

Shallow soil over chalk does not seem to bother ceanothus, cotoneaster, euonymus, forsythia, *Fuchsia magellanica*, lonicera, olearia and most roses very much, although good soil preparation undoubtedly helps the survival rate of other plants.

A dry but acidic soil is not generally popular but cotoneaster, indigofera, *Kerria japonica* and lonicera will do reasonably well.

For those who garden in towns or cities particularly, it is cheering to know that there are quite a few, particularly glossy evergreen plants, that will stand some degree of air pollution. *Camellia japonica* and C. × *williamsii* are good examples of this, as are chaenomeles, cotoneaster, escallonia, *Euonymus fortunei*, forsythia, *Garrya elliptica*, *Kerria japonica*, *Magnolia grandiflora*, mahonia, *Olearia* × *haastii*, pyracantha, most roses, together with hedera and parthenocissus.

Climbing plants are not happy on very cold and exposed sites, and wall shrubs even less so. Almost the only 'climber' that seems indifferent is *Euonymus fortunei*, although cotoneasters and pyracanthas will survive.

I should not like to give the impression that choosing wall and climbing plants is simply a matter of finding plants that will 'do'. Nothing could be further from the truth. As I hinted in the Introduction, the wonderful thing about walls is that they give the opportunity to grow plants that have not a hope of surviving a winter in an open position. These plants, the tender exotica from other lands, are some of the most beautiful that we can grow and, although we may never be able to achieve effects such as are seen in the favoured National Trust gardens of the south and west, we can try our luck with a variety of impressive climbers, including *Clianthus puniceus*, *Solanum jasminoides* 'Album', *Desfontainea spinosa* or *Crinodendron hookerianum*. Walls give us the opportunity to treasure some stunning, but otherwise impossible, plant, quite regardless of whether it 'goes' with anything else or not.

CREVICE PLANTS

No account of wall plants would be quite complete without at least a nod in the direction of those plants that grow *in* rather than on or against walls. This is rather more natural gardening than most concerned with wall plants, because, with or without our help, plants will find a niche there. Not all walls are suitable homes for what are known as crevice plants, of course; the better the condition of the wall, the worse are the chances of encouraging their colonization. It is in old-established walls, where the mortar has begun to degenerate, or where there is no mortar at all, that a few small plants may be insinuated without too much difficulty. The only chance of growing these plants in new walls is to build them with specially-made holes. Fortunately, the making of raised beds, which can be gardened by elderly or disabled people, is currently enjoying a vogue.

Especially suitable are those walls that retain the soil of a border. This is because, although there are some crevice plants that will survive on nothing more nutritious than stone dust, most need at least some nutriment and the opportunity of getting their roots into soil. After all, even alpine plants do not grow entirely out of the living rock; they usually have roots that extend a long way into rocky soil.

Some plants are obvious candidates for crevices and will, indeed, seed themselves in walls or the cracks of paving, if allowed, once introduced to a garden. Wallflowers are aptly named and two alpine bellflowers, *Campanula poscharskyana* and C. *portenschlagiana*, are well-suited to this habitat; valerian and *Phygelius capensis* will also establish themselves without any help from us. All can be rather invasive plants because they have the will to survive in adverse conditions. However, it is also possible to establish plants that are not naturally wall plants, such as the small hebe 'Carl Teschner', in a dry stone wall. Near where I live, *Tropaeolum polyphyllum*, (a yellow-flowered, grey-leaved relation of nasturtium) has been successfully established in shallow rockwork in a garden wall. Such examples as this may not always survive, but, for the pleasure of having colourful rock

CREVICE PLANTS

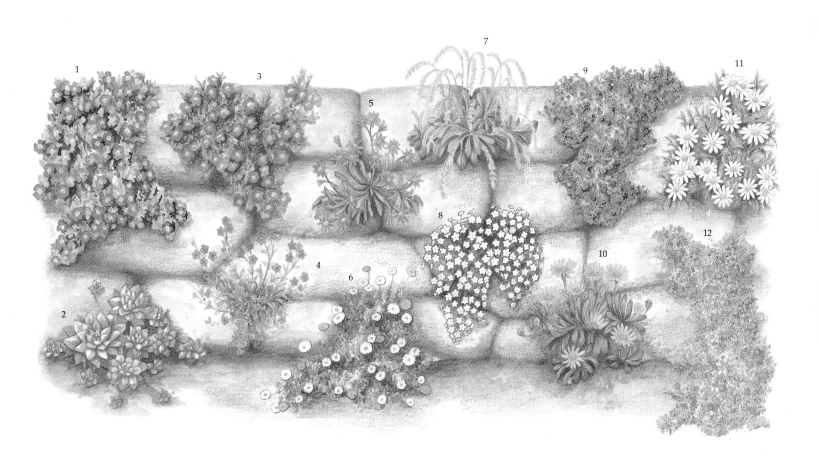

1 *Aubrieta deltoidea*
2 *Sempervivum*
3 *Helianthemum nummularium*
4 *Erinus alpinus*
5 *Lewisia cotyledon*
6 *Erigeron karvinskianus*
7 *Chiastophyllum oppositifolium*
8 *Saxifraga longifolia*
9 *Campanula portenschlagiana*
10 *Othonna cheirifolia*
11 *Anthemis punctata cupaniana*
12 *Lithodora diffusa*

plants in spring and early summer, it is always worth persevering.

BODNANT is well known for the variety of its crevice plants, which colonize the walls of the three terraces below the house. Appropriately enough, the Welsh poppy, *Meconopsis cambrica*, in both its orange- and yellow-flowered forms, is at home there, as is the very pretty purple-blue *Campanula portenschlagiana* and the pretty pink and white wall daisy, *Erigeron karvinskianus*. Even the white Japanese anemone has found its way into cracks in the steps near the Lily Pond. By far the choicest, however, are the different coloured forms (white, pink and rose) of *Lewisia cotyledon*, a plant that often suffers from neck rot if grown on the level. This is not an easy plant to establish, but it certainly looks very happy and associates beautifully with another plant not often seen in a wall, *Lithodora diffusa* 'Heavenly Blue'.

At UPTON, Sarah Cook, the former Head Gardener, managed to establish a drought-resistant, rather tender rock plant, with paddle-shaped grey leaves and yellow daisy flowers, call *Othonna cheirifolia* (syn. *Othonnopsis c.*), on a south-facing low wall. This is imaginative, because one of the features of slightly tender plants is that they are likely to be more resistant to frost in dry conditions than they are in wet. Also in the walls there can be seen varieties of sedum, as well as aubrieta, the hart's tongue fern, valerian, lemon balm, *Lithodora diffusa*, *Alyssum saxatile citrinum*, erigeron, helianthemum and *Armeria maritima*.

At COLETON FISHACRE, close to the sea in Devon, on a baking semi-dry slate terrace wall, masses of *Erigeron karvinskianus* vie for a place with pink fuchsia, cotoneaster, and even prunella.

Also suitable for a sunny wall are sempervivums (the house leeks, which can go on top of the wall, too) and saxifrages. I hesitate to mention the varieties of aubrieta, because the combination of purple-mauve aubrieta and yellow alyssum is often overdone. The most spectacular plant that I have seen in a wall was *Romneya coulteri*, the Californian tree poppy, which had somehow found its way into the brickwork of the South Cottage at SISSINGHURST. If it was anywhere but SISSINGHURST one might have thought it a happy accident, but it seems unlikely considering that it was growing next to *Rosa laevigata* 'Cooperi', which has a similar shaped white and yellow flower, earlier in the year. Also at SISSINGHURST is the choicest of bindweeds, the deep pink *Convolvulus althaeoides*, growing seemingly from nowhere out of the edge of paving on the Tower steps. *Euphorbia characias wulfenii*, *Convolvulus cneorum* and wallflowers can also be found growing in walls at SISSINGHURST.

It should not be thought that only south walls have their crevice habitués. North walls too have their share of candidates, of a rather different kind, it is true. Principal amongst these are the small ferns: the charming rusty-back fern, *Ceterach officinarum*, which is naturalized in many walls in Britain; the dainty *Asplenium trichomanes*; and the more robust hart's tongue fern, *Phyllitis scolopendrium*. Also happy in a shady spot are those relatives of the African violet, *Ramonda myconi* and *Haberlea rhodopensis*. Dwarf ivies will do very well, as will *Mazus reptans*, a hardy perennial that makes a creeping mat and has lilac flowers in summer.

Although it is often difficult to establish crevice plants, once they have got away they may flourish all too well. *Campanula portenschlagiana* and *C. porscharskyana* are well known for their thuggish tendencies, but the red valerian is also rampageous. Weeds also establish themselves in walls: buddlejas may be beautiful garden plants, much loved of butterflies, but they can survive on the walls flanking stations on the London Underground, so there is no reason why they should not find a way into garden walls too. Nettles and elder, which do not pretend to be anything other than weeds, can also soon find a toehold when your back is turned.

The best-known and most dependable crevice plant, *Aubrieta deltoidea*, flowing down steps at Snowshill.

PERGOLAS, ARCHES AND OTHER SUPPORTS

As I hinted in the Introduction, the usefulness of climbers goes far beyond their willingness to be trained against walls. Indeed, restricting them to walls is like growing tomatoes exclusively for sandwiches. There are, in fact, many climbing plants, such as rambling roses, that positively benefit from not being put against a wall and many more that can be shown off to as good, if not better, advantage elsewhere.

Pergolas, arbours, pillars and arches offer the best supports for climbers away from walls or fences. They are usually no good as shelterers, of course, unless built close to a house or garden wall, so must be planted with reliably hardy plants. However, they have their own particular assets. Twining and climbing plants, especially those with nodding flower heads, look very well against them; these supports are usually in the sun and plants around them generally suffer much less from water shortage than those on walls. Such structures are also usually more accessible for maintenance and they allow a much freer passage of air – particularly important in the case of rambling roses, which almost invariably contract mildew in the still atmosphere of a wall.

As far as the practicalities go, pergolas are usually made out of treated timber or brick pillars, which support treated softwood timber or ironwork horizontals, or can be bought,

LEFT A harmonious selection of pink roses, supported and free-standing, at Mottisfont. *Rosa* 'Debutante' and 'Bleu Magenta' ramblers are trained on arches.

RIGHT A pergola stretches the entire length of the Rose Garden at Polesden Lacey. Over it grow several specimens of just a few selected pink, white and red ramblers, including the highly scented 'Sanders' White Rambler'.

Ramblers also suit arbours and bowers, although their habit of flowering only once in the summer is a disadvantage in smaller gardens.

ready to assemble, in treated softwood. Arches are made of timber or wrought-iron, or you can now buy them in pieces for self-assembly, in timber or a strong plastic. Wrought-iron will need to be made to measure by a local blacksmith, if you are lucky enough to know of one nearby. Much use is made in Trust gardens of simple 'rustic' poles, of softwood, stripped of its bark, tied together to form tripods. These are available from some timber merchants. A simple structure of your own design can be easily erected; wires stretched horizontally will help tendril climbers to climb easily. Whatever you use, treat it first with plant-friendly preservative.

PERGOLA PLANTING

Choosing climbers for pergolas, pillars, arches and arbours requires thought. Many are ruled out by virtue of their tender disposition. Others need a shady spot and, with the exception of the (highly successful) pergola at BARRINGTON COURT, few pergolas are built close to a north-facing wall. Many more plants are not shown off to any particular advantage. It is well to consider carefully the advisability, or otherwise, of planting those climbers that have sufficient leaf, particularly evergreen leaf, to cause problems with rain-drip in autumn and winter. Vines may look very well on a pergola, and may remind you of a blissful summer holiday in Italy, but, unless you can avoid walking under the pergola in the wet season, the idea may rapidly lose its charm. The ornamental vine arch at POWIS CASTLE works well, with its contrasting underplanting of golden marjoram, but, as it goes nowhere in particular, there is no necessity for walking under it. The same is true of the famous Laburnum Arch at BODNANT, which can be easily avoided in rainy weather. Gardeners find climbing annuals very helpful because they can ring the changes each year, and they are not faced with the problem of winter drip.

As a general rule, plants with nodding or pendulous flower heads, such as *Rosa* 'Climbing Lady Hillingdon', or the hybrids and cultivars of *Clematis viticella,* look well on a

A Mediterranean atmosphere is imparted to the very English garden at Chartwell in Kent, by the use of vines over the Loggia.

pergola, and also those that are clothed (or can be encouraged to be clothed) well to the base. Those of slender growth habit (like the tender annual climbers) and those that can take hard pruning are better bets than heavy plants that cannot easily be curbed in this highly restricting situation. Alternatively, plants like *Akebia quinata* or *Actinidia kolomikta* that do not need a lot of pruning, should be chosen, because climbing up above a pergola on a cold day to prune is not everyone's idea of fun.

Evergreens may drip in winter but some, such as ivies, have the advantage of clothing the pillar and base of the pergola, and of giving colour all year. It is worth going for the rather weak-growing ones such as *Hedera* 'Green Ripple', 'Ivalace', 'Buttercup' or 'Goldheart', if trouble is to be avoided later on. *Euonymus fortunei* 'Silver Queen' is another possibility.

These climbers need not all be evergreen, of course. Low-growing honeysuckles such as *Lonicera* × *brownii*, sweet peas, and the everlasting pea, *Lathyrus latifolius*, are useful for the same purpose, as are pillar roses such as 'Paul's Lemon Pillar' and 'Compassion'. If you are going to use the not-too-vigorous large-flowered clematis, like 'Lasurstern' or 'Marie Boisselot', which flower both on the previous season's and this year's wood, you will have to prune them hard in the spring and lose the first flush of flowers. There is no alternative if the development of woody stems is to be avoided.

Truly vigorous plants may look wonderful on a pergola but they can be a headache to maintain. *Humulus lupulus aureus* looks marvellous, clothing a pillar to the ground, and forming a skirt onto the path under the pergola at BARRINGTON COURT, but it was described to me in 1990 by the Head Gardener, Mrs Christine Brain, as a 'bit of a pain'. One can see why.

In warm gardens, some fun can be had with plants not usually thought of as climbers. For example, at PENRHYN CASTLE, which benefits from the warm air above the Gulf Stream, the ogee wrought-iron arches that run almost the

The distinctive ogee wrought-iron arches at Penrhyn Castle run almost the width of the Walled Garden.

width of the Walled Garden from east to west, are planted with *Fuchsia* 'Riccartonii'. The pendulous deep red flowers look marvellous with the deep violet-purple *Clematis* 'Jackmanii Superba' when they are both flowering in July. Both can be cut down almost to the ground in February.

A list of suitable plants to climb up and over pergolas would include *Abutilon megapotamicum*, *Actinidia kolomikta*, *Akebia quinata*, *Asarina erubescens*, *Campsis radicans*, *Clematis*, *Cobaea scandens*, *Eccremocarpus scaber*, *Ipomoea tricolor* 'Heavenly Blue', *Jasminum officinale* and *J. nudiflorum*, *Lonicera*, *Passiflora caerulea*, rambler roses, vigorous climbing roses such as 'Maigold' and 'Madame Alfred Carrière', *Vitis coignetiae*, and *V. vinifera* 'Purpurea', *Solanum jasminoides*, *S. crispum* 'Glasnevin', *Tropaeolum peregrinum*.

RIGHT: Climbers with nodding or pendulous flower-heads such as wisteria and *Robinia hispida*, are perfectly suited to growing up arches, as here at Greys Court.

CLIMBING PLANTS

1   *Rosa* 'Albertine'
2   *Lonicera periclymemum* 'Serotina'
3   *Clematis montana rubens*
4   *Cobaea scandens*
5   *Jasminum officinale*
6   *Asarina erubescens*

CLIMBING PLANTS

7   *Passiflora caerulea*
8   *Akebia quinata*
9   *Rhodochiton atrosanguineus*
10   *Schisandra rubriflora*
11   *Vitis vinifera* 'Purpurea'
12   *Humulus lupulus aureus*

An English yew hedge plays host to the Chilean 'flame creeper' *Tropaeolum speciosum*, in late summer.

Only those of moderate growth are suitable for arches, arbours and pillars; unless, that is, the arbour is really substantial, like the one in the White Garden at SISSINGHURST, which can happily support a rose of the extreme vigour of *Rosa longicuspis*.

NATURAL SUPPORTS

Pergolas and arches are by no means the only kind of support available in the open garden: evergreen hedges provide an excellent host for some fragile climbers. *Tropaeolum speciosum*, the scarlet-flowered climber which does so well in Scotland, can be seen clinging to yew hedges at HIDCOTE and SISSINGHURST from midsummer, and *Eccremocarpus scaber* does the same thing in the Kitchen Garden at TINTINHULL.

Tree stumps have traditionally served as supports for not-too-vigorous climbers. *Clematis macropetala*, or one of its excellent named varieties, such as 'Markham's Pink', is ideal for this. If the stump is tall or the dead tree not yet removed, a vigorous and colourful climber such as *Vitis coignetiae*, *Celastrus orbiculatus* or *Humulus lupulus aureus* would be glorious. At PENRHYN CASTLE, honeysuckle is trained to help disguise a short conifer stump. The rather bushy climbing rose, 'New Dawn', would also be suitable, because it appreciates just that little support that a stump can provide.

Living trees should not be overburdened with very vigorous and heavy climbers, unless they are sturdy but, as has been shown at SISSINGHURST, for example, moderate roses, such as 'Madame Plantier', do well in fruit trees in the orchard. At MOTTISFONT, rose 'Ferdinand Pichard', competing with mistletoe, climbs through an old apple tree. Most spectacular is the *Rosa longicuspis* which falls in a white cascade from the top of a yew tree at PECKOVER in June, and the similarly vigorous and single white rose 'Wedding Day' from a tall holly tree at GUNBY HALL.

Since the autumn hurricane in Britain in 1987, many gardeners still have fallen trees in their gardens; these can be clothed with horizontal climbers until they are taken away or they rot, which may be many years from now.

A happy combination of sturdy pine and delicate clematis 'Gravetye Beauty' showing the rich beauty of this moderately vigorous *Clematis texensis* hybrid.

The immensely vigorous *Rosa mulliganii* in the centre of the White Garden at Sissinghurst. This is not a rose for the average-sized garden or timid gardener.

There are instances when it is desirable to enhance the appearance of an existing plant. I am thinking particularly of evergreen shrubs or conifers that begin to look rather 'samey' after the initial interest is over, particularly if planted in a prominent position. An unexpected outburst of flowering from a climbing plant growing through a conifer, say, can give a boost to an otherwise rather dull piece of garden. The clematis fits the bill nicely, for they are happy to have their roots in shade and are rarely too vigorous. I could envisage, for example, *Clematis × jackmanii* or *C. viticella* growing through one of the blue-green conifers such as *Juniperus horizontalis* 'Wiltonii'. The same effect can be achieved using late-flowering clematis or the everlasting pea, *Lathyrus grandiflorus*, through spring-flowering heathers, cultivars of *Erica carnea*. At HIDCOTE, in the Courtyard, *Clematis alpina*, which flowers in late spring, scrambles through *Schizophragma hydrangeoides*, which is a dull green until it bursts into flower in July.

More substantial plants need substantial support: for example, at TRERICE, *Jasminum humile* 'Revolutum' is to be found pushing its way through a mature 'Brown Turkey' fig. The great thing about using plants in layers is that, in small gardens particularly, it is possible to use a wider range of plant material than first appears justified, without overfilling the space.

At POWIS, there is in use some old wrought iron hoops, called 'Jackman hoops' after the famous Woking clematis breeder. These consist of eight arches, joined at the top, which give ample support to vigorous clematis such as *C. macropetala*, without human help, and at the same time give height to the border, without obscuring the plants trained against the wall.

Effective use has been made, in several National Trust gardens, of rough wooden poles to act as vertical supports for climbers. At HARDWICK HALL in Derbyshire, for example, the two forms of hop, *Humulus lupulus* and *H. l. aureus*, grow well up a wigwam of poles, held together with tree ties, in the Herb Garden. Nearby, in the east-facing border in the orchard, a system of three wooden poles, joined at the top and bottom with wooden crossbars, with wire stretched round horizontally at intervals, allow several clematis varieties to scramble. A similar arrangement of hazel poles and twigs supports clematis in the Iris Garden at BARRINGTON COURT. At ERDDIG, single rustic poles seem sufficient for clematis and rambling roses to climb to two metres or so in the Victorian Garden, while at SISSINGHURST, a wigwam of poles allows *Clematis* 'Alice Fisk' to flower in front of *C.* 'Madame Julia Correvon', which is trained to the west wall behind. These posts need not be wooden: at TINTINHULL, concrete posts are used to support vigorous specimens of the honeysuckle, *Lonicera japonica* 'Halliana' at the corners of the paths in the Kitchen Garden. Simplest of all, but effective, is the wigwam of canes, tied round on the diagonal with whippy hazel shoots, to support sweet peas, in the same garden.

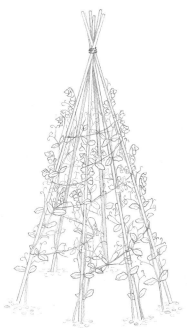

A 'wigwam' of bamboo canes tied at the top makes an ideal support for twining sweet peas.

TWENTY TOP CLIMBERS

In order to help you establish your own collection of wall plants or expand the stock you may already have, I have put together a list of my twenty top climbers. For a more extensive range see the Checklist on page 93.

NB *All heights and spreads are approximate, because the growth of a plant depends on its provenance, situation, aspect, soil, and feeding regime.*

1 *Abutilon × suntense*

This is a beautiful semi-evergreen shrub, which flowers in great abundance in May, June, and sometimes July. The flowers are mauve, five-petalled, flat, and measure about 50mm/2in across; they are borne in clusters from the leaf axils. The grey-green leaves are palmate, three-lobed, and pointed. A little hardier than its two parents, *A. ochsenii* and *A. vitifolium*, *A. × suntense* grows quickly to about 2.5m/8ft tall and 2m/7ft across, or a little more in favoured districts. It likes a south or west aspect and a well-drained, not too fertile soil. Although not long-lived, this shrub is self-supporting and the only pruning required is the removal of frosted or dead shoots in late spring, although the tipping back of shoots will help make a bushier shrub in the early stages. It has an even more striking variety with darker flowers called 'Jermyns', which, unfortunately, is not easily available from plant suppliers.

Abutilon × suntense has mauve flowers and grey-green leaves.

2 *Actinidia kolomikta* (Kolomikta vine)

Actinidia kolomikta is a handsome and unusual deciduous twining climber, closely related to the kiwi fruit, *Actinidia deliciosa* (syn. *A. chinensis*), and growing to about 4m/12ft in time. Although it produces small white male flowers in June, its main glory is the colour of the leaves. These are heart-shaped, up to 150mm/6in long, toothed, and, at the terminal end, white, gradually flushed with pink and silver.

The popular Clematis montana rubens *is one of the most amenable of clematis, and should not be forgotten.*

The colouring is particularly good in the early summer and if the shrub is grown against a sunny wall. However, it will grow in partial shade, if sheltered from cold winds, and provided it has some support from wires it can be grown up walls, over pergolas or into trees. Pruning consists of thinning out superfluous growths and tipping back others in late winter. That is also the time to layer the plant, if new plants are required. *Actinidia kolomikta* also provides an excellent background for purple- or glaucous-leaved shrubs.

Actinidia kolomikta has unusual leaves which are green with tips which become flushed with pink and silver.

3 *Camellia* × *williamsii* 'J.C. Williams'

Camellias are amongst the most popular of all shrubs which benefit from being grown against a wall, and the range is enormous. As attractive as any, in my view, are the × *williamsii* hybrids, such as 'J.C. Williams', because they shed their faded blooms. 'J.C. Williams' has single, cup-shaped, blush-pink flowers with yellow stamens, which appear from February until May. The leaves are glossy, dark green and ovate in shape; this shrub is more spreading and pendulous in habit than many camellias, being usually about 2 × 2m/ 7 × 7ft. The best aspects for it are west, north-west or even due north. The soil should be moist and enriched with organic matter. You can propagate camellias by taking semi-ripe or leaf-bud cuttings in summer, or by layering in autumn.

4 *Carpenteria californica*

This is a shrub worthy of a place in any garden that can provide a little shelter from cold winds, for it is reasonably hardy, in the south and west at least, and is stunning when the white fragrant, anemone-like flowers, with yellow stamens, first appear in June. Even out of flower it is handsome because of the glossy-green lanceolate evergreen leaves. The flowers have up to seven petals and are 70mm/3in across. The shrub grows to about 2m/7ft with a 1.5m/5ft spread, which means that it can be grown against a bungalow or other medium-sized wall. It likes a well-drained, but not too dry, soil in a sunny, sheltered position. It can be propagated by cuttings, layers, or seed sown in spring.

5 *Ceanothus* 'Delight'

Ceanothus is one of the few shrub genera with proper blue, as opposed to mauve, flowers, and is practically indispensable. *Ceanothus* 'Delight' is one of the best of the hybrids, which are a little hardier than the species. It is evergreen and vigorous (growing up to 3m/10ft and as much across) with deep green, oval leaves and 70mm / 3in long panicles of bright blue flowers in April and May. Like other ceanothus, this one does best in a sheltered sunny position, in a light soil. Ceanothus tend not to be long-lived and there is always the possibility of loss in a hard winter, but you can propagate them quite easily by taking semi-ripe cuttings in July and putting them in a little heat. Once flowered, the shoots should be trimmed.

6 *Chimonanthus praecox* (wintersweet)

Of all the winter-flowering shrubs, *Chimonanthus praecox* smells the sweetest, hence its common name of wintersweet. It is a deciduous, hardy and bushy shrub, which grows to a maximum of 3 × 2.5m / 10 × 8ft. It is not fussy as to soil, although it has a slight preference for an alkaline one, and does best in a sunny place. However, even in ideal conditions, it may take a few years before it flowers. The leaves are shiny and mid-green in colour, lanceolate and about 100mm / 4in long. The 25mm / 1in wide flowers hang their heads and are almost transparent; they consist of long green-yellow, outer segments, and shorter purple inner ones. The flowers appear on the naked stems from very short pedicels between December and February. This shrub can be grown in the open, but is usually found against a house-wall, where the scent can be appreciated without too much of a winter trek. Stems can be cut for the house, and the bells will open in water indoors but, as the shrub is not fast growing, most gardeners find it painful to cut much of it for this purpose. Pruning consists of cutting back flowered shoots to within a few inches of their base. There are two cultivars, 'Grandiflorus' and 'Luteus', whose names are self-explanatory.

7 *Cistus ladanifer* (sun rose)

The entire cistus (sun rose) tribe, being of Mediterranean origin, appreciate the warmth and shelter afforded by a

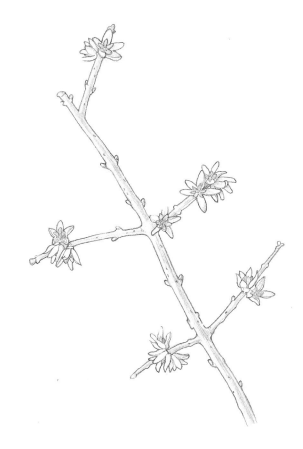

The flowers of the highly-scented tender wintersweet *Chimonanthus praecox* have yellow outer and purple inner petals, borne on the naked stems in January and February.

sunny wall. They are particularly useful as short, evergreen shrubs to plant in front of a bare-stemmed climber like *Rosa* 'Mermaid' or clematis. One of the best, and hardiest, is *Cistus ladanifer*, which produces its clusters of large (20mm / ¾in across) bright white flowers, with a thin purple-red blotch at the base of each petal – like a careless blood-splash – and a boss of yellow stamens in June and July. Like all cistuses, these flowers are delicate, with five thin petals, which open in the morning and are shed by the evening. The shrub's habit is basically erect, with some arching branches. The leaves are green, leathery and lanceolate. Cistuses do best, and flower most freely, in a poor, stony soil in full sun, sheltered from cold winds. They can be propagated by sowing seed in March in pans or pots put in a cold frame. No pruning is necessary, besides removing dead and frosted shoots, if any, in spring.

Cistus ladanifer bears bright white flowers with a thin purple blotch at the base of each petal and a boss of yellow stamens at mid-summer.

8 *Clematis flammula*

Of all the genera that climb by twining, the genus *Clematis* must be the largest and most versatile. Because so much hybridizing has been done with a variety of clematis species, there is now an enormous range to choose from; depending on the cultivar they will also flower from early spring until late autumn. One of the very best is *Clematis flammula*, not only because its myriad white flowers come late on in the season for a species (August until October), but also because they smell deliciously of almonds. It is a vigorous climber, which can reach 4 – 5m / 13 – 16ft tall, and so can be trained up or along a wall or into a tree. It will grow in any aspect and is none too fussy about soil, although, like all clematis that are related to old man's beard, it has a preference for alkaline soils. It should be planted where its roots have a cool, shaded root run. As it tends to go bare at the base, most of the bushy growth being towards the top, try to plant an evergreen shrub in front of it. It is not easy to propagate from cuttings; seed should be sown in the autumn, or layers in the spring. Pruning consists of cutting most of the stems right down to about 300mm / 1ft from the ground in late winter, leaving only a few which can flower early on (see page 82).

9 *Clematis* 'Lasurstern'

Clematis 'Lasurstern' can be taken as representative of the many large-flowered clematis that start to flower at or before mid-summer, on wood made the previous season, and therefore need to be treated differently from the later-flowering ones (see page 82). 'Lasurstern' is best planted in a shaded position where the deep purple-blue flowers will not fade too soon to a washy pale mauve-blue. The flowers have seven or nine sepals and are some 150mm / 6in wide. They come out in May until July, and again in September. This plant grows to about 3m / 10ft high.

10 *Cytisus battandieri* (Moroccan broom)

It is not just the scent of fruit salad which is so appealing about the flowers of the Moroccan broom; it is the shape and size of the flowers themselves. They are a clear yellow, in broad, cylindrical racemes about 100mm / 4in long and stand out from the silvery green trifoliate leaves on the lateral shoots in June and July. The flowers are followed by

50mm/2in long seed pods. Although hardy, this most handsome semi-evergreen shrub (which can reach 5m/15ft tall in a favoured position) undoubtedly flowers best in a warm, sheltered sunny place. If necessary, remove two-thirds of the lateral shoots after flowering.

alone, even if it did not have large, flat flower-clusters with pretty white sterile flowers in June, attractive peeling bark, and good (yellow) autumn colour. It neither needs much pruning (except perhaps removing any damaged shoots in spring) nor a rich soil, although it prefers it not to be too dry. The self-clinging habit is possible because of aerial adventitious roots, although it will need a little encouragement to begin with to get it going where it is wanted. This plant does not flower when very young, and is inclined to sit for 18 months or so before it begins to grow away. Once begun, however, it will reach up to 15m/49ft eventually, if permitted.

The fruit-salad scented cylindrical racemes of the Moroccan broom, *Cytisus battandieri*, are bright yellow.

11 *Hydrangea anomala petiolaris*

There is no more useful wall climber than *Hydrangea anomala petiolaris*. Its habit of clinging unaided to anything from a fence to a rough-barked tree commends itself to gardeners, as does its capacity to thrive (and flower well) on sunless walls. Indeed, we should probably still grow it for those virtues

Hydrangea anomala petiolaris has white flowers and leaves which turn a pleasant yellow in autumn before they fall.

12 *Jasminum humile* 'Revolutum' (jasmine)

There are several excellent hardy jasmines for growing on walls, and one of these is the yellow-flowered *Jasminum humile* 'Revolutum'. Scented and free-flowering, it is hardy and evergreen, and requires little attention because it is only semi-scandent. It can be grown free-standing, although it does grow well trained against a wall. The soil need not be very good; all that is required is a position sheltered from cold winds. The leaves are a leathery dark green, divided into leaflets, and in summer the yellow flowers are borne in clusters up to 150mm / 6in long.

13 *Lathyrus odoratus* (sweet pea)

The sweet pea is probably the best-loved of all climbing plants, grown for the sweetness of its scent and the beauty of its keeled flowers in summer. Sweet peas can be grown as individual plants on bamboo canes (this is called the cordon system and is the method employed by flower show exhibitors, and also Paul Underwood, Head Gardener at PECKOVER HOUSE), up fences, netting, tripods, against walls, and through shrubs. The subject of attention for plant breeders, amateur and professional, for well over a hundred years, the colours now range from white to very dark purple, with waved or straight petalled flowers, about 25mm / 1in across. In the newer 'Spencer' varieties, scent has sometimes been sacrificed to flower size. The gardener can suit himself when ordering from seedsmen, choosing either from the 'Spencer' cultivars or the older, smaller, generally more scented 'grandiflorus' types. The seed is best sown in October (earlier in the colder north), overwintered in a frost-free frame, and planted out in March once hardened off.

The sweet pea has distinctive leaflets in pairs, which are ovate and mid-green in colour, and end in a tendril, enabling the plant to cling to a support. Flowering usually begins in June and can continue until the end of September, particularly if the flowers are picked regularly to prevent the seeds in the feathery silver seedpods being set. This plant needs a sunny aspect to flower well, preferably sheltered from cold winds, and in a well-drained but fertile and deeply dug, slightly alkaline, loam.

14 *Lonicera × italica* (honeysuckle)

The climbing honeysuckles can offer both scent and flower colour over an extended period. These attributes more than make up for the fact that they present an irresistible temptation to the black bean aphid. *Lonicera × italica* is a vigorous hybrid between our own naturalized *L. caprifolium* and a beautiful Mediterranean species called *L. etrusca*. It has oval leaves and many large panicles of yellow, flushed purple, and very fragrant flowers in June and July. Cuttings do not present a problem if taken from semi-ripe wood in summer; layers also work if put down in autumn. This deciduous honeysuckle does not require a lot of pruning unless planted in a very restricted place; any thinning out should be done after it has flowered. Because honeysuckles are woodland plants, they should at least have their roots in shade.

15 *Parthenocissus henryana* (Chinese Virginia creeper)

The best known so-called Virginia creeper is *Parthenocissus quinquefolia*, but a better plant, to my mind, is a close relation, *Parthenocissus henryana*, because of the striking variegation that the leaves exhibit from the start of the growing season. The leaves turn to bright red in autumn, have three or five oval leaflets, anything from 40 to 120mm / 1½ to 5in long, and these are either bronze or dark green, with the main veins pink, white or purple. This variegation is particularly obvious if the plant is grown in a shady place. As it is not entirely hardy in all districts, it enjoys a north- or north-east-facing wall, although it can also be grown up fences, over pergolas, and against the trunks of rough-barked trees. This climber clings by means of the sticky pads on the end of tendrils. After planting, it is helpful to pinch out the leading shoots to encourage the plant to branch, but, once established, it does not need much attention, unless it outgrows its space.

16 *Rosa* 'Climbing Étoile de Hollande' (climbing rose)

Impossible as it is to avoid bias in the choice of roses, gardeners generally agree that one of the finest climbing roses is 'Climbing Étoile de Hollande'. This is a climbing sport of a hybrid tea rose introduced in 1931. The flowers are deep red, semi-double, with loose petals and golden anthers, and a rich scent. They are also repeat flowering. Growing to about 4m / 12ft high, this is a good rose for a pillar or a wall. The expression 'climbing rose' is slightly misleading as roses scramble using the barbed thorns on their stems; they therefore need help, in the way of wires and string, to bind them to their support. Rose like 'Climbing Étoile de Hollande' are best pruned in late winter, by removing old, dead and diseased wood, tipping back vigorous young shoots, and cutting flowered laterals back to two buds or so from the base.

17 Rosa 'Gloire de Dijon' (Noisette rose)

Roses need a well-drained, fertile soil in a light position, if possible, but some will tolerate less than perfect conditions. One of these is 'Gloire de Dijon' (the old glory rose), which will grow quite well on an east or even north wall. It is a beautiful rose, with very fragrant, large, quartered buff flowers, suffused with apricot, and even pink in warm weather. Quite vigorous, growing up to 5m / 15ft in good conditions, it is one of the first roses to flower, yet repeats well into the autumn. Most roses (with the exception of species and ramblers) are not easy to propagate, except by budding, which is normally beyond the scope of the amateur gardener, so they are best bought bare-rooted or root-wrapped in the autumn, or in pots in the spring.

Schisandra rubriflora is an attractive climbing shrub with small crimson flowers in late spring.

18 *Schisandra rubriflora*

Although not a startling shrub in flower, *Schisandra rubriflora* is, nevertheless, a handsome and garden-worthy plant, particularly as it flowers in late spring, before the roses and clematis. It can be used in any of the situations that suit the latter and, although generally hardy, benefits in cold districts from being trained against a wall. It will thrive in a semi-shaded place, indeed it is best out of direct sunshine. It has twining stems but needs some encouragement to climb when first planted, so horizontal wires will need to be in place. Schisandra is happiest in a slightly acid soil, but will grow in lime provided you add plenty of humus. If planted against a wall, it is susceptible to drought, so you need to mulch it each spring. It grows to about 4m / 12ft, has obovate leaves and unisexual flowers. These are bowl-shaped, about 25mm / 1in wide, deep crimson, smell of raspberries and hang from the leaf-axils in April and May. A well-grown, mature plant is quite a sight. Schisandra requires no pruning as a matter of course, although, if there are a lot of shoots coming away from the wall, these can be removed in winter. Take cuttings in summer but, as they do not root very readily, it is advisable to place them in a propagating case with bottom heat provided.

19 *Vitis coignetiae* (Japanese crimson glory vine)

Vitis coignetiae is by universal acclaim the best of all ornamental vines. It can (although mostly it does not) grow to 25m / 75ft tall, which means that it is ideally suited to climbing into tall deciduous trees. It can also be used (as it is at SISSINGHURST and HIDCOTE) to grow along or over walls. This is a much more acceptable vigorous plant for hiding an ugly garage than *Fallopia baldschuanica*. It is deciduous, with woody stems and huge heart-shaped leaves, rough in texture, up to 250mm / 10in long, with five pointed lobes. These are dark green above, and ruddy-brown beneath. It flowers in June and July, producing insignificant green grape flowers, but it is grown for the magnificent autumn colour of its leaves, particularly if planted in the sun. This can range from purple to deep red, orange and yellow. It should not be allowed to dry out (an easy occurrence if it is growing up a large thirsty tree), for the leaves will be smaller and will fall earlier. Although this plant, like all vines, has tendrils, it will need initial encouragement to climb by the use of string or netting. If space is restricted or you do not want the entire area swathed in vine, shorten the young shoots in summer to deter growth; otherwise it can be left to its own devices to twine at will.

20 *Wisteria floribunda* 'Multijuga' (Japanese wisteria)

There are several varieties of wisteria available, ranging in colour from deep purple ('Black Dragon') to pure white (*W. sinensis* 'Alba'). My favourite, because of the extravagant nature of the flowers, is *W. floribunda* 'Multijuga'. It is a vigorous plant, growing up to 9m / 27ft, has 12 to 19 leaflets, and the racemes of scented lilac-blue flowers grow up to 1.2m / 4ft long. Wisterias are shown off to the best advantage on a pergola where the racemes of flowers in May and June can hang down. On a wall that possibility is lost and there is always the chance that the long curling shoots will start to lift the roof tiles. Wisterias need pruning twice a year: once in July, when the current season's long laterals are cut back to about 150mm / 6in, and again in February, when these are shortened still further to about three buds from the base of the shoot.

As well as pergolas, wisterias will grow against trees, over arches and on walls and fences. They can even be trained as weeping standards. They like the sun but will tolerate some shade and they flower best in a not too rich soil. Indeed, the gardeners who complain that wisterias are slow to flower are often at fault for planting them in a rich soil, although sparrow damage or cold weather at bud formation time will also have unfortunate consequences. Wisterias can be propagated by layers put down in May or heel cuttings taken in August and given some bottom heat.

Wisteria growing in the gardens at Trelissick.

GROUND PREPARATION AND PROPAGATION

The important point to remember about the cultivation of wall plants is that whatever you do must be done especially well. Wall plants are subject to more stresses than those that affect the same plants in the open and, in particular, they are more likely to suffer from drought and malnutrition.

It is not difficult to see why. The soil close to a house is likely to be poor, and may even be almost non-existent. Wall plants are often very vigorous, either naturally so, or because they enjoy the shelter afforded by the wall, and will therefore demand more from the soil than the average shrub. They will also, in probability, live in the same place for many years.

At OXBURGH HALL, preparation of the planting hole for a wall plant is taken very seriously. Graham Donachie, the Head Gardener, believes in digging out and abandoning the old, stale soil, particularly if there is any likelihood of replant disease, such as occurs when one rose is replaced by another. He will dig out a section at least 600mm/2ft deep, 750mm/2½ft along the wall, and 375mm/15 in out. He forks up the base of the hole, then puts back a mixture of fresh soil, leafmould and bonemeal. The point of such labour is to give the wall plants a flying start and help the soil retain moisture. This may seem like hard work to the average gardener (and can certainly be said to be the counsel of perfection) but, particularly in the case of vigorous and greedy climbers such as rambling roses, it may be justified. Too many climbing plants are left to eke out an unthrifty existence, flowering little and grudgingly, and prone to pest and disease damage, because not enough care has been taken with the soil in which they must grow.

In order to stiffen the sinews and summon up the blood to do this, it is helpful to make the leap of imagination and visualize the roots of a long-lived plant like wisteria growing out for several metres, searching for water and nutriment. If you can do that, you will see that it makes sense to plant your wall shrubs towards the back of a border, rather than just in a hole in the paving; in that way, mulches can be laid on each spring, and the plant watered if necessary. The only exceptions to this are those plants, such as clematis, that thrive best if their roots have a cool root run, particularly if they are planted in a sunny spot.

In an ideal world, preparing the planting hole should be done some months before planting, in order to give the planting mixture time to settle. If this is not possible, allow for the fact that there will, in time, be at least a centimetre of settlement, when planting your shrub.

In ordinary circumstances, a hole 450 × 450 × 450mm/ 18 × 18 × 18in is fine, provided you fill it with a mixture of good soil and whatever else you have to hand such as mushroom compost, well-rotted farmyard manure, leaf mould, or home-made compost. The more fibrous the organic matter the better, because moisture retention in summer is usually important for most wall plants, except a few shrubs that prefer a poor dry soil, such as cistus. Most wall shrubs are not happy in a heavy clay, so add sharp grit to help aerate it. Add 110g/4oz of bonemeal per bucket of planting mixture to help stimulate root growth.

The importance of good ground preparation to promote a thriving plant and generous flowering cannot be overstated.

There is no longer a consensus that peat is a useful ingredient of planting mixtures, which is just as well since there is now anxiety about the depletion of raised peat bogs to serve gardening purposes. You may feel the use of peat is justified if you wish to grow a spectactular but lime-hating (calcifuge) plant such as *Crinodendron hookerianum* or *Berberidopsis corallina*, but it is not advisable unless your soil is already on the acid side of neutral, when amounts used in the planting mixture, and later as a mulch, need only be quite small.

If you have not already done so, now is the time to secure wires to the wall, if necessary; this is a task very difficult to do successfully once climbers are in place but worth taking time and care over.

PLANTING OUT

When to plant depends not only on the plant, but how it has been grown. If it is in a pot, theoretically it can be planted at any time of the year; in practice, container-grown plants are best planted in mid to late spring, especially if they are rather frost-tender, as many wall shrubs are. 'Tender' in this context also includes those plants that have young shoots vulnerable to frost damage in spring; hydrangeas, for example, are mostly hardy in this country but still their spring shoots are very easily blackened by night frosts. September or October is an alternative time for planting, especially suitable for hardy stock. I should not advise summer planting, unless substantial watering is easy to arrange and likely to be carefully carried out.

Bare-rooted deciduous plants can go in at any time in the dormant season (early November until early March), so that is the time to plant roses, trees, fruit trees and bushes, dug out of nursery fields, or any plants given to you from a friend's garden.

I have written earlier about the intelligent choice of climbers, but here it is pertinent to say that it matters almost as much how good a specimen you buy as the species itself. Climbing plants are usually sold in containers, and should

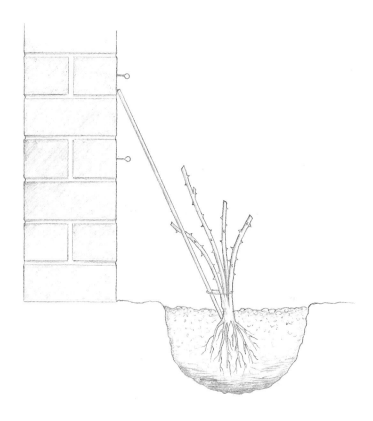

When planting wall plants against a wall, do not forget to take the 'rain shadow' into account, by placing the shrub at least 300mm / 12in from the wall. A bamboo cane is useful to help direct growth.

therefore be inspected to see that they have not been long enough in the pot for the roots to girdle, or too short a time for the roots to have pushed out into the new compost. If you feel an (understandable) reticence about checking these important details for yourself in the garden centre, ask an assistant to do it for you, and do not buy the plant if it is either pot bound or only very recently potted. Plants with frosted (brown and shrivelled) shoot tips or much dead growth in them should also be shunned, as should any with a pest population or an obvious disease problem.

Planting follows the same routine as with any shrub, except that, because of the rain shadow that exists even on garden walls, the plant should ideally be placed about 300-450mm / 12-18in in from the wall. If it is a climber, lean it gently against the wall. Retain the bamboo from the pot to support fragile climbers, at least until they have 'got away'. Most bare-rooted plants have an obvious mark on the stem that denotes the level at which they were planted before; see that they are planted (allowing for a little settlement) at the same level again. With container plants it is the compost level that is the guide. Of the two, too deep planting is marginally worse than too shallow, except with roses where too shallow planting gives the chance for suckers to become a nuisance, and clematis, which should be planted deeply in case they 'wilt' (see page 86 on pests and diseases). Once the 'soil' has been trodden down, the area should be well watered. If the ground has been very dry, this will easily 'run off', in which case watering the hole (and, of course, the plant in the container) well first is a better option.

Incidentally, many climbing plants, particularly if not correctly pruned, have rather bare 'legs' and so, ideally, should be planted at the back of a border with shrubs and perennials in front to hide their nakedness. These smaller shrubs should not, however, be planted so close to the climber as to prevent the sun reaching the stems and ripening the 'wood' for the following year's flowering.

I shall be discussing pruning of individual shrubs later but here it is worth saying that many wall shrubs need some initial pruning after planting. This is because it is so important to establish a balanced plant, with a good framework of stems, whose buds face sideways rather than outwards. Any dead, diseased and twiggy wood should also be removed.

Most climbing and rambling roses will need their main shoots cut back to between 230 and 450mm/9 and 18in from the base after planting. The exceptions to this are those roses that are climbing sorts of bush roses, such as 'Climbing Iceberg', which may revert to bush form if pruned really hard at the beginning. Pillar roses that flower on the current season's wood need no initial pruning either.

With wisteria, the idea is to establish lateral growths: cutting back the main stem after planting to about 1m / 3ft should stimulate the growth of these. With ceanothus, it is a matter of only retaining those shoots that are well-placed to grow sideways. Vines are cut back hard after planting, to within two buds of the base. Clematis are cut back to the lowest pair of strong buds as they begin to 'break' in late winter, at least for the first two years.

Crevice plants can be a little tricky to establish. If you are building a wall, it is a good idea to rake the wall back slightly, and leave 75mm / 3in square holes, irregularly on different courses, which can be filled with a gritty compost.

There are several ways of planting crevice plants. Ideally, put them in as the wall is being made, although the two operations are not easy to synchronize. If holes have been made, remove them from their pots, squeeze the roots gently into the shape of the hole and with a few small stones plug any gap to prevent the soil coming out (illustration overleaf).

If there are no man-made holes, you can poke some out of the mortar, or, in the case of a dry stone wall, ease the stones away slightly. Whatever you do, use either small plants or seed wrapped up in a plug of soil. Large plants may suffer root damage as they are being squeezed in and will, in any event, have a larger requirement for water initially. All newly-planted crevice plants will need to be kept moist and well-watered.

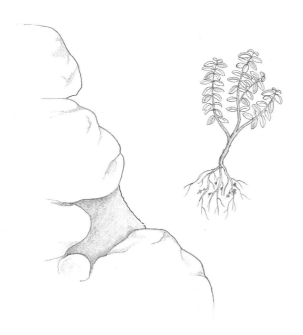

Crevice plants such as *Helianthemum*, should be planted by squeezing their roots gently into a hole in the wall, with a little soil to fill any gaps.

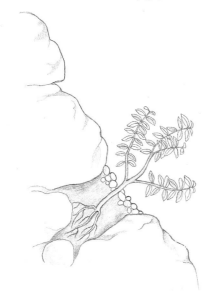

A layer of stones helps prevent this soil from falling out.

PROPAGATION

From time to time, it is necessary, or desirable, to increase wall plants and climbers by propagating from existing stock. This may arise because the plant is in the wrong place and will not survive transplanting; because it is short-lived (ceanothus, for example, does not last more than a few years); because it is tender and is very unlikely to survive the winter; or simply for the fun of having young plants to give to friends.

The tender annual climbers such as morning glory, *Asarina erubescens*, *Cobaea scandens*, *Eccremocarpus scaber*, and *Rhodochiton atrosanguineus* need to be sown in a free-draining seed compost in pots in early spring. Cover them with newspaper and put them in a windowsill propagator, or warm, dark place. Once they have properly germinated, they should be pricked out individually into at least 100mm / 4in pots and gradually hardened off in May before being planted out, when danger of frost is past. They all require some sort of support, such as a thin stake, at least until they get a fingerhold on wall wires. They will need water until obviously well established.

Climbing hardy annuals, such as the sweet pea, *Lathyrus odoratus*, are sown in pots put in a cold frame in October, and protected against the worst of the winter weather. They can be hardened off in March before being planted out.

As for perennial plants, propagate them by cuttings, by layering or, in the case of species, by seed (although this is not very usual, because it is so comparatively slow).

Depending on the plant, you can take cuttings when softwood in early summer, semi-ripe in mid-summer, or hardwood in the autumn. Clematis, for example, are often propagated by 'internodal' softwood cuttings, that is, cuttings that are cut between, not at, the place where the leaves originate. Plants with long or fleshy extension growths such as *Coronilla glauca*, *Fuchsia magellanica*, or the runner growth of hedera can be taken as nodal softwood cuttings in early summer; these are taken at about 50 – 90mm / 2 – 3.5in long, and put in a pot of cuttings compost

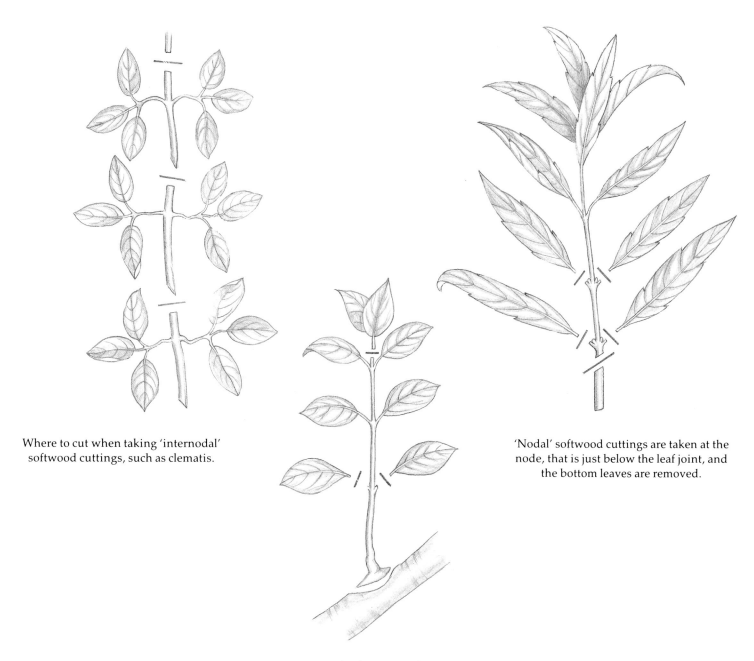

Where to cut when taking 'internodal' softwood cuttings, such as clematis.

'Nodal' softwood cuttings are taken at the node, that is just below the leaf joint, and the bottom leaves are removed.

A semi-ripe shrub cutting taken with a 'heel' of older wood. This is suitable for, amongst others, pyracantha and ceanothus.

A suitable receptacle for cuttings: a pot filled with half peat and half sharp sand, covered in clear polythene kept off the cuttings by hoops of fine wire.

(50 per cent coarse sand, 50 per cent peat), which is then enclosed in a clear polythene bag, to stop moisture loss until the cuttings have rooted. A spray with a fungicide such as benomyl is advisable.

Most wall plants that are shrubs can be taken as 75 – 120mm / 3 – 5in semi-ripe cuttings in mid or late summer. These are usually best taken with a 'heel' of older wood still attached. Some species strike more readily if they have a source of heat below them, provided usually by soil-warming cables in sand on the bench in the greenhouse. Abelia, actinidia, campsis, ceanothus, chaenomeles, choisya, escallonia, evergreen lonicera and vitis, all strike best in this way. Many others, such as rambler and species roses, can be taken at this time, without bottom heat.

Hardwood cuttings are taken in autumn and are suitable for a variety of easily-propagated shrubs, such as cotoneaster, hedera, deciduous honeysuckles, and *Ribes speciosum.* They are usually longer, between 150 and 250mm/6 and 10in and are put in a slit trench, into which has been dribbled some coarse sand.

Layering is a useful method for those shrubs with stems flexible enough to be brought down, without breaking, to ground level. Here, the underside of the stem is slit and the stem pegged to the soil, or to a sunken pot filled with cuttings compost, with flexible wire. Clematis, particularly, respond well to layering; so-called 'serpentine layering' sometimes works when internodal cuttings do not. The young stem is laid in curves on the ground in June, and

Layering is an easy method of propagating shrubs with flexible, or ground level shoots, such as jasmine. The stem is cut on the underside and pegged to the soil until it roots.

'Serpentine' layering can be successful as an alternative to internodal cuttings with plants such as clematis.

A difficult subject such as *Magnolia grandiflora* can be successfully 'air-layered'. A slit is made in a stem, covered with damp sphagnum moss and tied with soft string.

This should be covered with an airtight, clear polythene covering. When roots are seen to have formed, the branch can be cut below the layer and planted.

should have taken some root by the autumn. *Magnolia grandiflora* can be 'air-layered'; that is, a slit made in a young shoot, which is covered with damp sphagnum moss, held in place by soft string, and covered with an air-tight clear polythene sleeve. (See page 72 for propagation requirements of many wall plants.)

SUPPORTS

With the exception of the self-clingers, all wall climbers will need some kind of support. Many, like clematis and sweet peas, are naturally twiners; others, like roses, use their thorns to scramble over other plants; others still are simply shrubs that naturally grow in open places and are being squeezed against a wall or fence for their own protection or our appreciation of their trained appearance.

Fortunately there are as many kinds of support as there are kinds of wall plants so, in theory at least, it is possible to find something to suit. You will need to decide whether thin trellis nailed to battens and secured to the wall with screws and wallplugs is what you require, (i.e. for clematis and other delicate twiners) or galvanized wire (1.6mm gauge for preference) attached to vine eyes or masonry nails banged into mortar or drilled into bricks. This is another job that must be done well, for nothing is more infuriating than wires coming adrift under the weight of a large (and usually thorny) rose.

Generally speaking, National Trust gardeners seem to prefer stout galvanized wire for brick and stone walls, at 450 or 600mm / 18 or 24in intervals, stretched horizontally and tautly between adjustable straining bolts. You can also use masonry nails with eyes but they have no device for tightening the wire and, as anyone will know who has tried it, wire has a will of its own, particularly when first uncurled from a reel. Masonry nails are, however, useful for banging into the mortar in a place halfway between straining bolts, and then passing through the wire to help keep it straight.

Occasionally, between large windows where wall-space is limited, these wires are stretched vertically as well, which suits twining plants like clematis. It is not sensible to rely entirely on vertical wires, however, for fragile climbers may simply fall down them into a heap.

Plastic-coated wire is also available, and is usually green, but you can also buy brown plastic large gauge clematis netting that can be secured to walls with special wall clips, in turn screwed into wall plugs. Least satisfactory, in my opinion, is chicken netting or green plastic pea netting, particularly if put against a wall or fence. It works best when stretched between two simple wooden posts to provide a structure for sweet peas or runner beans to climb in the vegetable garden.

Cheaper, and more informal support can be given with pea-sticks or similar material. At ERDDIG, for example, birch twigs are used, leant against a wall, for the perennial *Lathyrus grandiflorus* to climb and, in the same garden, a clematis finds support by clinging to a thin, cut, tree stem with branches which have been tied to the wall wires.

Most gardeners are faithful to garden string as the best means of tying up wall climbers. In the case of large or vigorous climbers, such as roses, tarred string is preferable, because it will last a season, whereas the ordinary string may not. In some instances, such as keeping large magnolias fixed close to walls, wire, cushioned with a piece of old water hose, should be used, or even pieces of strong cloth. The trick is not to allow anything to bite into the bark of the plant as it expands with age, because the thin column of food-conducting cells is situated just behind the bark and damage to it will cause the plant to starve. When quick and repeated tying is needed for fast growing climbers such as cobaea and clematis, thin paper-coated wires, call 'plant-twists', are ideal. They are as easy to remove as they are to put on, but they should not be thought of as a substitute for string where substantial climbers are concerned. Plastic, unperishable ties, that can be adjusted depending on the size of stem to be caught, are also available. The ones known as 'heavy climbing supports' can be hammered into masonry and then tied round a shoot.

PRUNING AND MAINTENANCE

One of the more enjoyable features of growing wall plants, as far as I am concerned, is the intellectual effort required to maintain them properly. That may seem a contentious sentiment, but I do not believe that the fun of gardening resides solely, or even principally, in planting something and forgetting about it ever after. To me, pruning a well-trained rose well is as satisfying as finishing a crossword puzzle, and almost as mentally taxing. In this section I shall take a variety of commonly planted wall plants and explain their pruning and training regime.

Many shrubs require little or no pruning as a general rule. However, if they are to be trained against a wall they will need to be pruned to prevent them spreading out in all directions as they would naturally like to do. This is particularly true of chaenomeles or ceanothus. Most climbers need little or no treatment if they are allowed to grow up a tall tree, as they would in nature, but they must be pruned if grown on a wall, pergola, pillar, arch or tripod.

The point of this kind of pruning, beyond the obvious and universal one of getting the best balance between flowering and vegetative growth, is to restrict the plant to the space allotted for it. Pruning is not entirely straightforward, some plants being rather idiosyncratic in their requirements. However, you must first grasp the general principle that some shrubs (mainly those that flower in the first half of the year) are flowering on 'wood' made in the previous year,

Chaenomeles are usually grown as a fan of main branches with some laterals left to fill in gaps, and all the outward-growing shoots cut back hard, preferably after flowering.

some (those that flower after midsummer) are flowering on wood made in the current season, and some (like some clematis) flower first on old wood and then on new, as the season progresses. Then you will not go far wrong!

For example, these plants, such as *Forsythia suspensa*, which flower in the spring, should have their flowered laterals (sideshoots) cut back to within 25 or 50mm / 1 or 2in of their base. Those which flower in late summer, such as *Buddleja crispa*, can have their long shoots cut back very hard to the new shoots, but in late winter, just before they burst strongly into growth. Vines should be pruned in the middle of the dormant season, because they 'bleed' sap so readily otherwise. Tender evergreen shrubs such as *Carpenteria californica*, ceanothus, even camellia, are best left to their own devices and simply trimmed if they are outgrowing their site. Any pruning should be done in the spring, rather than the autumn.

If National Trust gardens are representative of the nation's gardens, the rose is the most commonly planted wall shrub of all. Not only at MOTTISFONT, the garden specifically given over to roses, do they form the staple coverers of walls. Roses are, unfortunately, not without their inherent difficulties: not only are they mightily thorny but, in order to flower well, they need to be pruned in a thoughtful way.

There is not much dispute about the timing of pruning climbing and rambling roses: ramblers, being once-flowerers that flower on last year's wood, are dealt with after flowering, whereas climbers can be pruned any time from late autumn to early spring, often depending on when there is time. At MOTTISFONT for example, where rose pruning is one of the most important maintenance tasks, David Stone, the Head

When pruning ramblers in late summer, remove most old
flower shoots near the base, cut back the laterals to about
two buds, and tie in the new shoots.

Do not cut back vigorous ramblers so hard. Retain some
old wood, cutting back the rest only as far as strong newer
shoots. Remove flowered laterals.

When pruning repeat-flowering climbing roses in autumn
or early spring, remove very old wood and cut back all
flowered laterals to two buds from the main shoots.

Prune pillar roses according to vigour. Cut in the autumn if
growing beyond the pillar; prune out the flowered laterals
after the first and second flush.

Gardener, likes to see them tied up in the autumn, to stop wind damage, and pruned in spring. At UPTON, Sarah Cook (Head Gardener until 1990 and now at SISSINGHURST) favours the winter because there is no harm done at that time by putting ladders on the wall borders.

Good practice dictates that you should untie the roses and take them down from their supports. Cut out all dead, diseased, and damaged wood together with a proportion of the very old stems (exactly how much depends on the amount of new replacement growth the rose has made). Then cut back the old flowered shoots to about three buds, tie the new young stems in and tip them back if they are too long for their position.

The controversy begins with the tying in. Most skilled gardeners tie roses (and indeed many deciduous wall shrubs) neatly into the fan shape, without any crossing pieces. This is an extension of how they prune bush roses: so that there are no chafing stems and so that light can reach all parts. That seems sensible but there are problems with it as a method because, as the flowers tend to appear towards the end of the stems made in the current season, the 'legs' of the rose become increasingly bare. This matters little if there is plenty planted in front, or if the wall is tall enough but, if neither is the case, the lower sparseness is very noticeable.

At SISSINGHURST and at UPTON a more imaginative method prevails. The flowered stems are cut out, as usual, but many of the rest are tied in horizontally or even arching downwards, even if this means crossing them over other stems. Placing the main stems horizontally not only encourages better flower production (the slower the sap stream the better the flowering) but also means that those flowers clothe the wall better because they begin lower down.

The balustrade roses are quite strictly dealt with at UPTON: the flexible young shoots naturally arise from the crown of the plant, which is in a bed below the wall; these are bent over the top and are tied in, everything else being cut out. The act of bending over these shoots naturally encourages a lot of flower buds to break.

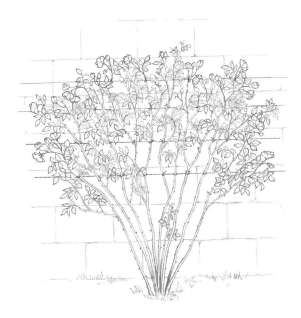

A traditional fan-trained rose, tied diagonally to horizontal wires.

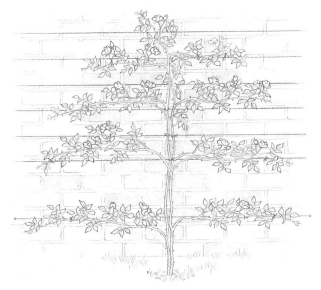

A vigorous rambler rose can be trained as an 'espalier'. If the horizontal shoots outgrow their space, they can be turned and brought back.

At PECKOVER HOUSE, Paul Underwood recognizes the same principle but solves the problem in a slightly different way. He trains the long growths of vigorous ramblers such as 'François Juranville', on the wall in the Pond Garden, horizontally, in an espalier shape, and, if the stem reaches beyond the end of the available wall space, he turns it round and brings it back again just below. It looks neat, works well, and is fitting in this Victorian garden.

The mention of clematis pruning is enough to make strong men blench, but it is not complicated if you know the flowering time of the clematis you intend to prune. Clematis belong, broadly speaking, to three groups as far as pruning requirements are concerned. **Group 1** are mainly spring- and early summer-flowering species, or cultivars from species, and can be pruned after flowering, with the removal of dead and damaged wood and the cutting back of too strong growths. **Group 2** are mainly those early summer, large-flowered hybrids, like 'Bees' Jubilee' and 'Marie Boisselot', that flower both on last season's growth and later on the

Spring-flowering clematis (**Group 1**).

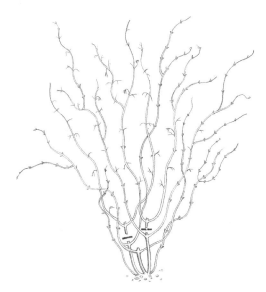

Early summer-flowering large-flowered clematis (**Group 2**).

Clematis such as the Jackmanii group (**Group 3**).

current season's wood. Some, but not all, of last year's growths are cut back in late winter, as far as the highest pair of strong buds which are showing. Finally, **Group 3** are those, like the Jackmanii group, that flower after midsummer on growth made in the current season; all stems are cut back hard, to about 300mm / 12in from ground level in late February or early March. Examples of clematis in this group include 'Perle d'Azur' and 'Hagley Hybrid'.

If you forget to carry this out one year, a thunderbolt is unlikely to come down from the sky and strike you on the head; the clematis will still flower, albeit rather more messily. Species clematis can, in many situations, be left alone; Sarah Cook says she has a 'live and let live' policy with these, unless they are trained on a wall.

However pruned, as the clematis grows, the quickly lengthening stems need to be encouraged to grow where required to give a good-shaped plant. Plant twists are ideal for this. As far as pruning other wall plants is concerned, provided some general points are remembered and a certain amount of common sense is exercised as to individual needs, you will not go far wrong. Firstly, it is necessary to establish a framework of branches, particularly for sturdy wall shrubs such as chaenomeles, and to try to make a well-filled shape. Secondly, those shrubs that naturally wish to grow in all directions will need to have their outward-growing shoots cut back, because they are so difficult to tie in. Cut to a sideways or upwards facing bud. If you are going to prune, try to do deciduous plants in the autumn and evergreen subjects in the spring as they are often more tender. When in doubt do not prune into good wood, simply remove dead, damaged and obviously diseased wood.

Throw the rule book away if you are pruning those spring flowering plants that have berries, such as pyracantha. In normal circumstances you would prune after flowering, but it is unwise to do so very conscientiously or you will lose too much of the fruit. Better to prune lightly then, and lightly again in the autumn.

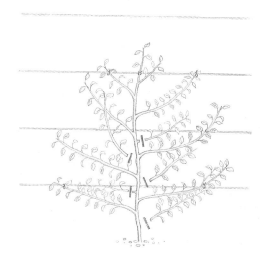

In their first summer, evergreen ceanothus can be pruned by removing some laterals, particularly outward-growing wood; the other laterals and the terminal shoot are then tied in.

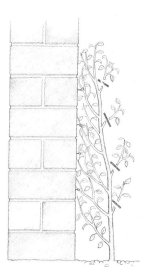

In their second summer all flowered laterals should be cut back.

Pruning and training climbing plants on other structures than walls (for example, pergolas, pillars, tripods and arches) is much the same, except that it is even more important to try to encourage replacement growth towards the base of the plant.

FEEDING; PEST AND DISEASE PREVENTION

One of the paradoxes of growing wall climbers is that you have to feed them well to keep them growing healthily in often less than ideal conditions, but, when they do grow well, you have to remove so much of that growth. Do not be put off by the irony, however, because unfed wall plants can often look rather sickly and their flowering may be affected. That said, it is marvellous how some wall plants can exist without what looks like any of the richer things of life: there is, for example, a substantial *Indigofera heterantha* growing out of a crack in the paving on the terrace facing west at Kiftsgate Court in Gloucestershire.

It seems to me only fair to give your wall shrubs a yearly sprinkling of balanced organic fertilizer, such as fish, blood, and bone, in spring. This can be scattered round the plant, at a rate of 70 grams per square metre / 2 ounces per square yard and scuffed in with a hoe. This provides nitrogen, which is taken up quickly and helps manufacture chlorophyll in the leaves, phosphates for root growth and potash for flower and fruit development. Seaweed is another good general organic fertilizer, rich also in minor and trace elements such as iron and magnesium. An inorganic alternative is a balanced general fertilizer such as 'Growmore'. Repeat-flowering roses, such as 'Climbing Iceberg', will benefit enormously from an additional boost after the first flush of flowers with a fertilizer, specially formulated for roses, such as I.C.I.'s 'Rose Plus'. Rose specialists such as David Stone at MOTTISFONT and Paul Underwood at PECKOVER give their roses two feeds: one before the main flush, and one after it.

A thick 75mm / 3in mulch of mushroom compost (provided the plants are not lime-haters), farmyard manure, leaf mould, bark chippings, or a recently introduced organic alternative to peat such as J. Arthur Bower's 'Mulch and Mix', put on after wet weather in spring, will help retain moisture in the summer, particularly in sunny spots. It is especially beneficial for those plants that enjoy a cool root run, while liking their flower heads to be in sunshine, such as honeysuckles. Fibrous organic matter, or what is sometimes known, incorrectly, as humus, has a cooling effect on the soil, because it helps it to retain moisture. It will also go a long way towards suppressing annual weeds, and make perennial weeds (if there are any) easier to pull out. At POWIS CASTLE, for example, the Head Gardener, Jimmy Hancock, believes in mulching all the borders each spring; the gardeners make up their own mix of a third good strawy manure, a third leaves, and a third one-year-old compost; it has a nutritional value, as well as the obvious virtues of moisture retention and weed suppression.

Plants that are fed and watered well will be less enervated by pest and disease attack than those left alone. However, nothing will save your plants entirely from attack, and it is as well to recognize that, before you plant anything that will require you to climb ladders to spray or risk getting an eye, nose and mouthful if you work from ground level. Walls, with their still, warm conditions, are ideal breeding grounds for a range of pests and even some fungi which, contrary to popular belief, do not only thrive in damp, cold conditions.

Of these, powdery mildew is the most widespread and debilitating, striking rambling roses such as 'Albertine' especially badly. Indeed so bad is it, that many gardeners avoid putting these roses on walls at all, preferring to use tree stumps or pergolas as hosts instead. Honeysuckle and clematis can also be affected by powdery mildew in hot, dry seasons. You can give some help by mulching well at the beginning of the growing season to keep the soil moist; otherwise spray with propiconazole, benomyl, or triforine.

The use of black-painted wooden trellis between the iron arches provides extra purchase for climbers, as seen here at Wallington.

Sensible too is the planting of reasonably resistant rose varieties: among climbing roses with a good record for health are 'Maigold', 'Paul's Lemon Pillar', 'Climbing Lady Hillingdon', 'Madame Grégoire Staechelin' (a very useful rose because of its ability to thrive on an east wall), 'Golden Showers', 'Madame Alfred Carrière' and even a rambler, 'Albéric Barbier'.

Roses are also affected these days by rose rust and, in wet seasons especially, by blackspot (so you cannot win!). The first shows itself as yellowy-orange pustules on the undersides of leaves in summer, with black pustules appearing as the season wears on. The second is characterized by dark brown spots that gradually merge and yellow the leaf that falls. Both are very damaging diseases that overwinter on affected leaves. Garden hygiene is thus very important, if rather impractical. Spray with propiconazole for both, or myclobutanil for rust.

Clematis are most at risk from so-called 'clematis wilt', strictly speaking 'clematis die-back'. This causes shoots to die back very rapidly, sometimes all the way down to the base, particularly on young plants. This die-back soon turns black. Not a great deal is known about the biology of this disease, but very often the clematis will recover the following season, if the affected shoots are cut out to below the point where the wilt has begun. The fungus may enter the stems through wounds, so take care when tying them, or hoeing close by. (If you have been a Wise Virgin and placed a few stones or tiles round the clematis this cannot happen of course.) The great clematis expert, Christopher Lloyd, recommends planting clematis deep, so that 30 – 50mm / 1 – 2in of the stem is buried. Then, if the clematis dies back, there is still healthy wood underground capable of shooting.

The recently restored Victorian Garden at Erddig has pillars planted with the rambler rose 'Dorothy Perkins' and *Clematis × jackmanii* which calls for skilful pruning in such a confined space.

Potentially even more damaging is the bacterial disease, fireblight. This is because it is capable of affecting most members of the Rosaceae family (roses, apples, pears, plums, peaches, cotoneaster, pyracantha, kerria and chaenomeles), and can lead to the death of the plant. Most likely to be affected on walls are cotoneaster and pyracantha. It causes leaves to wither to a brown paper in the growing season. Cut out and burn affected branches to a point about 100mm / 4in below where the damage has reached. This disease is notifiable so you will have to inform the Ministry of Agriculture.

The most damaging fungus of all because it can attack any woody plant is honey fungus. This is especially a problem in old-established gardens, where dead wood such as tree stumps remain for the fungus to live on saprophytically. The fungus spreads by means of 'bootlaces', called rhizomorphs, and will gradually infect any tree or shrub, particularly young or weak ones. If honey fungus is suspected, and especially if the 'bootlaces' are found underground or the distinctive honey-coloured fungi appear in autumn, the infected plant and a considerable area of soil around it should be removed. There is some doubt about the complete efficacy of the proprietary honey-fungus killers, but 'Armillatox' is worth a try. It may cheer you to know that clematis, among a number of trees and shrubs, appears somewhat resistant to armillaria attack.

Other diseases include coral spot, which has become so much more aggressive a fungus in recent years. It used to be seen almost exclusively as orange pustules on dead wood, but there are widespread reports that it is becoming more and more parasitic on woody plants. Amongst wall shrubs, magnolias and pyracanthas are likely to be affected, but Paul Underwood at PECKOVER has had trouble with coral spot on a 'Brown Turkey' fig on a wall in the 'cutting' garden. Burning all affected wood quickly seems the best method of defence.

Wall shrubs and climbers are especially unfortunate in their attractiveness to aphids, particularly greenfly and blackfly. This is because aphids, which suck the sap of plants, like the green young shoots that wall climbers, being rapid growers, often have in abundance. Some people despair of growing honeysuckles, for example, in sheltered warm places because they make such a tempting feast for blackfly. Another villain, the peach-potato aphid, loves roses, peaches and many other plants.

There are many types of aphid that the gardener may not have the time or inclination to identify precisely, but which he knows are harmful. They compound their felony by both encouraging the growth of sooty moulds by the secretion of 'honeydew', and by the transmission of viruses in their saliva. Amongst the viruses that debilitate wall shrubs and climbers are pea mosaic virus of sweet peas, cucumber mosaic virus of, for example, *Passiflora caerulea*, rose mosaic virus, tobacco mosaic virus on *Solanum jasminoides*, and wisteria vein mosaic virus. It matters little whether you can name these viruses; the important thing is to recognize that yellow veining, mottling, and crimpling of the leaves may be due to virus, so always keep aphids under control, and keep the area around treasured plants well weeded. If the plant is badly affected, it should be grubbed up and burned.

Other insects that can cause problems from time to time include caterpillars, sawfly such as rose leaf-rolling sawfly (especially on roses planted on walls in shade or semi-shade), capsid bugs, and thrips. A non-persistent organic pesticide, pyrethrum, will give short-term control of these.

Birds, by pecking or nesting, can cause damage to wall climbers while, more down to earth, slugs, woodlice and earwigs do damage at their base. Aluminium sulphate should see to the slugs, while pirimiphos can be used against earwigs and woodlice.

There are some other ills that afflict wall shrubs, but which cannot be put down to either pests or diseases, even if the damage bears a resemblance to them. I am thinking in particular of spring frost damage, and also nutritional deficiencies. There is little to be done about the first, as the young leaves must be left to develop unhindered by winter protection. Wall plants often come into new soft lush leaf

A fine display of 'Pink Perpétue' roses. Spraying is often necessary if you are to achieve healthy and floriferous blooms such as these.

earlier than the same plants grown in the open and, though walls give some protection from frost, there are occasions when they are not enough. This can affect the quality and quantity of flowering. The only thing to do is to be very careful about which aspect you site vulnerable plants such as hydrangeas. Curiously, ceanothus seem less affected by spring frosts than other, ostensibly hardier, plants.

Many plants are put against walls not because they like dry soil but because they need freedom from cold winds and harsh weather. Therefore, drought is often a problem and must be ameliorated with mulches and punctilious watering.

Wall plants are not immune to wind damage, either, especially in the spring when the drying easterlies are at their worst, and especially when the wind is not filtered and its force broken; susceptible subjects are ceanothus, jasminum, *Robinia hispida*, cistus and trachelospermum. The tenderer cistuses frequently give up the ghost in these conditions, having come through snow and ice unscathed.

Nutrient deficiencies can hit plants hard, if soil conditions are not ideal – and they often are not. Without annual mulches of organic matter, many plants will start to show chlorosis towards the end of the growing season, especially, but not exclusively, if they are lime-haters in neutral or slightly alkaline soils. Lack of iron and magnesium are the commonest deficiencies, and a dose of sequestered iron for the first, and Epsom salts for the second, usually does the trick nicely.

It is not all a litany of troubles, however: some wall shrubs are almost immune from attack, especially those invaluable evergreen shrubs such as *Garrya elliptica* and *Carpenteria californica*. Nothing much disturbs the even tenor of the ways of *Akebia quinata*, *Fremontodendron californicum* or *Piptanthus nepalensis* either.

PLANT RESUSCITATION AND WINTER CARE

I sometimes think that life would be easier if you could start from scratch when you moved into a new garden. However, it is often not to be and so you must do with what is there.

This may not be very much, perhaps no more than some unmown grass, weedy hardy perennials, and one or two neglected climbing roses. As far as the latter are concerned, it is an iron law that whomever you buy a house from will have subscribed to the Hack Theory of Pruning, which means that for years, every growth will have been cut off at a particular height with no consideration for the age of the wood.

It is unlikely that you will be able to tell what the rose is, unless it is flowering, for you have to be very sophisticated to know what kind of roses are growing by the shape of their foliage. Some people might manage 'Albertine' or, at a pinch, 'Albéric Barbier', but anything else is very difficult to identify. Fortunately it does not matter very much as far as remedial work is concerned.

The first thing to do, at any time of the growing season, is to cut out all dead and obviously diseased wood. You will need a pair of sharp 'parrot-bill' pruners or at the least a saw for this. Then pull out any suckers that are coming up from the roots; these will have different leaves from the rest of the plant. If the rose has obviously been left for many years and there is a great deal of dead and diseased wood, it would pay you to do this renovation over two seasons rather than all in one go. Pruning is, after all, a considerable shock to a plant's system and really drastic work may well kill off a neglected shrub.

When the plant is dormant in winter, cut any ties that are keeping the rose to the wall (as often as not wire that has been allowed to cut into the stems) and bring the stems out and, if possible, lie them on the ground. Then cut out about half of the main stems, unless they have some very strong shoots growing from them. These should be cut back to about three buds from where they arise from the stem. Tie back all the stems which are left. The following winter the oldest remaining shoots can be removed in the same way. After pruning, give the plant a good top dressing of organic material and, if it is still flagging the following summer, feed with a foliar feed, because there may have been root damage particularly where building work has been carried out.

Non-rosaceous wall shrubs can be dealt with in much the same way, except that evergreens should be pruned in late spring, if possible at the time when they are making new leaves, while deciduous plants can be cut back in winter. Again this may be done over two years. Some plants, such as *Cytisus battandieri*, do not take kindly to having their old wood cut into, but most will stand it if it is done in gentle stages. Again, feeding afterwards gives the plant heart to produce new strong growth.

It is harder to know what to do with a large shrub, say a magnolia, which has been neglected and come away from the wall. If it is not possible to replace the wires behind it and immediately pull it back to them, it may be possible to do it in several stages, using a cloth rag to secure it, which can be progressively tightened as the plant becomes used to being held taut once more. Otherwise, cutting the plant down hard, past the problem area, may be the only, if rather drastic, alternative.

As has been said before, we take a chance with many plants that are not naturally hardy in our climate by planting them against walls. However, even this may not be enough in harsh winters or if the plant is young with stems not yet lignified. That is why special winter precautions are sometimes necessary. Fortunately, these days, there is an excellent material for this purpose, available readily, namely a lightweight polypropylene shade and windbreak material. The great advantage of this material is that it has many air holes and will even let a limited amount of light through. This material can either be used on its own, round the stem of vulnerable plants, such as is done at BARRINGTON COURT, or can be tied to bamboo canes that are disposed round a shrub, to act as a three-sided shelter. If the gap inside can be loosely filled with straw (or dry bracken, if you live near a wood or heath) so much the better, because frost is far more damaging in damp conditions. This material has the added advantage of defending the plant from searing cold winds. It is not always possible, even using the windbreak, to protect a wall plant for more than a few feet of its height but, even if

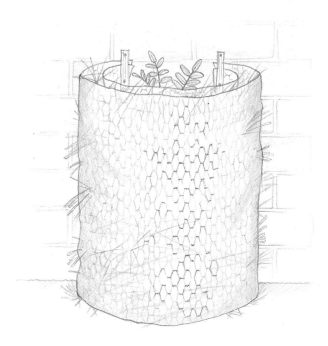

A roll of chicken wire, filled loosely with straw or bracken, will help see a tender plant through the
winter but it must be removed when growth starts in the spring.

the top is blasted by frost and snow, the base should be capable of shooting again. In some situations, however, a batten can be fixed horizontally above the shrub, onto which can be nailed windbreak material that then hangs down like a curtain. Alternatively, it can be held up there by long bamboo canes, onto which it is draped, and these leaned against the wall.

Polythene is an alternative but is even less attractive to look at and may encourage too humid an atmosphere inside it. Where polythene comes into its own is in protecting wall-trained peaches and nectarines from peach leaf curl, because the spores cannot germinate in autumn and winter if the conditions are dry.

Another tried and tested method is to make a kind of wire mesh Swiss roll: this consists of two tubular enclosures of chicken wire, between which is put straw or bracken. An easier alternative perhaps, perfectly adequate for tender herbaceous perennials, is 300mm/12in of wood ashes or coarse sand mounded over the crowns.

Winter protection should ideally be in place by the beginning of December, before the worst weather begins, and be taken off in March as the plant comes into growth once more. What must not be assumed, however, is that the placing of protective materials around vulnerable shrubs will mean that you can grow everything normally thought of as tender. It will merely help to protect those shrubs on the borderline of hardiness in cold districts, or more tender plants in favoured districts. Once a plant is well established, it may be possible to leave off winter protection. Although most gardeners see this task as something of a fag, not always justified by the severity of our winters, it is painful to lose a prized shrub because for some reason one has assumed that bad weather is a thing of the past.

Suitable subjects for protection in inland areas include *Abeliophyllum distichum* (the lower portion, for otherwise you cannot see it flowering in January and February), *Abutilon* × *suntense*, *Berberidopsis corallina*, *Buddleja crispa*, *Campsis radicans* (when young), *Carpenteria californica* (in exposed places), evergreen *Ceanothus*, tender species of *Cistus*, *Clianthus puniceus*, *Crinodendron hookerianum*, *Dendromecon rigida*, *Desfontainea spinosa*, *Drimys winteri*, *Fremontodendron* 'California Glory' (in cold districts), *Fuchsia magellanica* 'Versicolor', *Hoheria lyallii*, *Myrtus communis*, *Passiflora caerulea* (when young), *Pileostegia viburnoides* (until established), *Piptanthus nepalensis* (in cold districts), and also *Solanum jasminoides* 'Album'.

Fruit trees such as plums, gages, and peaches that flower early in the spring and that are trained against walls may be protected from threatening frost by spraying the flowers with a fine spray of water late in the evening. This technique, widely used by fruit farmers, freezes round the blossoms and protects them. The sun in the morning melts the ice first, so that the flowers do not heat up too quickly. Although this is not usually advised, this seems to me to be an acceptable device for protecting the flowers of early-flowering ornamentals such as *Abeliophyllum distichum* and *Chimonanthus praecox*.

However energetic you are about winter protection, you will have to accept that some plants are only to be seen in frost-free gardens. A plant growing at TRENGWAINTON or PENRHYN, does not mean that it can be grown elsewhere, even with winter protection. I have lost *Clianthus puniceus* on more than one occasion. Nevertheless, hope springing eternal in the human breast, I shall go on trying. If we are to have the undeniable beauty of many wall shrubs, we have to learn to be philosophers. One should give thanks that it is possible to plant tender perennials, such as *Eccremocarpus scaber* or *Tweedia caerulea* (syn. *Oxypetalum caeruleum*), and treat them as half-hardy annuals, ringing the changes the following year.

CHECKLIST OF WALL PLANTS AND CLIMBERS

The vital facts of more than 120 wall plants and climbers, which will help the reader make an informed choice, are given below.

'Tender' means that the plant will not withstand temperatures dipping below freezing point; 'half-hardy' means that it will not withstand temperatures below −5C (23F) for any length of time, and 'hardy' means that it can be expected to withstand even harsh winters. It is hard to be dogmatic because altitude, soil, moisture, exposure and snow-cover can all affect a plant's chances of survival. In general terms it is unwise to plant too great a proportion of species that are on the edge of hardiness in the garden for, even if they do not die in a hard winter, they will probably not flower well. The reader must be ruthlessly honest with him or herself about the garden's true conditions if there is not to be wasted time and money. That said, although the best soil and aspects are indicated, many shrubs will tolerate less than ideal conditions.

1 *Abelia* × *grandiflora* is a semi-evergreen, half-hardy wall shrub, with a height and spread of 3m / 10ft, which enjoys a south or west aspect in a well-drained soil. The leaves are glossy and the scented pink and white flowers tubular in shape. These are borne from July until October.

2 *Abeliophyllum distichum* is a deciduous, not very hardy wall shrub. It likes a sunny aspect and a well-drained but fertile soil. The flowers are star-shaped, white with a tinge of pink, scented and come out in January and February; the leaves are dark green, oval in shape, and appear after flowering.

3 *Abutilon megapotamicum* can be grown either against a wall or up a pergola; it is an evergreen, slightly tender shrub, which can grow to a height and spread of about 2.5 × 2.5m / 8 × 8ft. It needs a well-drained soil and benefits from winter protection. The flowers are pendant with yellow petals and red calyces; they are carried over a long period from May until October.

4 *Acca sellowiana* (**syn.** *Feijoa sellowiana*) is an evergreen, half-hardy shrub, which grows to 3 × 3m / 10 × 10ft. It likes a sunny aspect and light, well-drained soil, and will need winter protection except in very favoured districts. The leaves are dark green, and ovate with white undersides. The flowers are borne in June, and are large, dark red with white-edged petals; the fruits are edible, red-tinged green but are only borne if male plants are nearby.

5 *Akebia quinata* is a fashionable twining plant for a wall, pergola or tree. It is semi-evergreen in favoured districts and, though hardy, prefers a sunny aspect. The soil should ideally be moisture-retentive but well-drained. Its leaves are distinctive, consisting of five rounded leaflets. The scented flowers, which come out in late spring, are a curious brown-purple; they are followed by purple fruits the shape of sausages.

6 *Ampelopsis brevipedunculata* is a twining wall plant grown for the shape of its dark-green, three-lobed leaves and its ability to climb 5 m / 16ft or so up a wall. It will grow in either sun or partial shade. The flowers, which are green and inconspicuous, appear in June; they are followed by bright blue berries.

7 *Asarina erubescens* (syn. *Maurandya erubescens*) is a tender, twining annual, for a south or west aspect and a fertile, well-drained, humus-rich soil. Its use is for walls (as long as strings can be provided) or trellis. The leaves are triangular in shape and downy; the flowers are four-lobed, white outside, rose-pink inside, and 70mm / 2¾in long. They come out between July and September.

8 *Azara microphylla* is a scented, half-hardy shrub reaching 5m / 16ft or more, with glossy green rounded leaves and tiny yellow, petalless flowers in February and March. Winter protection is helpful initially but this species is hardier than other azaras. It does like a sunny aspect and a well-drained soil.

9 *Berberidopsis corallina* is a half-hardy evergreen, twining wall plant, which enjoys cool shade in a rich, free-draining lime free soil. If happy it will grow to 5m / 16ft. The leaves are oval to heart-shaped and leathery, edged with small spines; the flowers are globular, deep red and carried in drooping clusters from July until September.

10 *Buddleja crispa* is a tenderish and deciduous

wall shrub, which grows up to 3 × 3m / 10 × 10ft and likes a southerly or westerly aspect and a well-drained soil. It has attractive woolly white shoots and leaves. It has broad panicles of scented lilac flowers with white eyes.

11 *Camellia* **'Cornish Snow'** makes a tall, evergreen, half hardy shrub which likes a west-facing or even north-west-facing wall, and a lime-free, moisture-retentive soil. The leaves are lanceolate, bronze when young and then purplish brown. The flowers, which appear in March, are single and white.

12 *C.* **'Leonard Messel'** makes a shrub about 4m tall × 2m across (13 × 6½ft) and has semi-double, bright rose-pink flowers, 100mm / 4in across, from February until April.

13 *C. reticulata* **'Trewithen Pink'** is also evergreen and half-hardy, with a taste for a sheltered semi-shaded wall, and a damp, acid soil. It grows up to 5m / 16ft tall in good conditions and has dark green, elliptic and reticulate leaves, and large (150mm / 6in) semi-double, rose-pink flowers in late winter and early spring.

14 *C. reticulata* **'Mary Williams'** is much the same size and shape as 13 and enjoys the same conditions. The flowers, however, are single, deep pink, with obvious golden stamens.

15 *C.* × *williamsii* **'Donation'** has glossy green, ovate leaves, and semi-double, silver-pink, 75mm / 3in wide flowers, which are shed when they have faded. It is at its best between February and April/May.

16 *Campsis radicans* does well on a wall, fence or pergola. It is a vigorous deciduous climber, which clings by means of aerial roots. It can reach 12m / 40ft in height. It grows best in a sunny aspect and well-drained soil. It should be protected for its first two winters. The leaves are pinnate and light green in colour; 80mm / 3in

scarlet and orange trumpet flowers are borne in August and September.

17 *C.* × *tagliabuana* **'Madame Galen'** is an offspring of 16, and can be treated similarly. The trumpets are salmon-red.

18 *Ceanothus* **'Autumnal Blue'** is an evergreen and hardy wall shrub that thrives in a light and free-draining soil against a sunny wall. The leaves are large (about 25mm / 1in), glossy, and ovate; the flowers, which come in clusters, are small, and soft blue in colour. They appear from July until October.

19 *C.* × *burkwoodii* is also an evergreen ceanothus but not as hardy as 18. It also enjoys a sheltered, sunny wall in a light, free-draining soil. It has oval, glossy, dark green leaves and bright blue flowers in 50mm / 2in panicles at the same time as 18.

20 *C.* **'Cascade'** is similar, except that the leaves are narrowly ovate, and the 60mm / 2½in panicles of small, powder blue flowers come out in May and June.

21 *C.* × *delileanus* **'Gloire de Versailles'** is deciduous, hardy, and usually 2 × 2m / 6½ × 6½ft in height and spread. Its leaves are mid-green, ovate, and larger than most ceanothus. The flowers are also large: 200 mm / 8in long panicles of soft powder blue, scented flowers from June until October.

22 *C. impressus* is a large, half-hardy wall shrub with small, deep green, glossy leaves closely packed on the stems. The flowers are in clusters, about 30mm / 1¼in long and deep blue. This beautiful shrub flowers in early summer.

23 *C. thyrsiflorus repens* makes a prostrate evergreen shrub, very useful to trail over a low wall. It is one of the hardiest of the ceanothus, although it does appreciate a light free-draining soil and a sunny sheltered spot. The leaves are

Although Japanese quinces can be grown in the open, they have most charm when trained well against a wall of hand-made bricks.

deep green, oblong and glossy, and the flowers are light blue and borne in 75mm / 3in clusters in May and June.

24 *C. × veitchianus* is a large (3m / 10ft), evergreen, hardy wall-shrub, with obovate, toothed leaves, and 50mm / 2in clusters of small bright blue flowers in May and June.

25 *Chaenomeles speciosa* **'Moerloosei'** is a deciduous and hardy wall-shrub, which can attain 3 × 3m / 10 × 10ft. It likes any ordinary soil,

except for a shallow chalk one, and will grow on any aspect, although it prefers sun. The leaf is dark green, glossy and ovate; the apple-blossom flowers in small clusters are pink-flushed white and carried between January and April. The fruits are quince-like, and a greenish-yellow.

26 *C. speciosa* **'Nivalis'** closely resembles **'Moerloosei'** except that the flowers are pure white.

27 *C. × superba* **'Rowallane'** is a deciduous,

wall-shrub, which grows to 75mm × 2m / 3in × 6½ft. It tolerates most soils and aspects. The flowers are large, semi-double and red; they are borne from March until May. The fruit is yellowish-green.

28 *Choisya ternata* **(Mexican orange blossom)** is an evergreen, half-hardy shrub that makes a big, mounded shrub, about 2 × 2.5m / 6½ × 8ft. It will grow in sun or partial shade, although it needs a sunny aspect in northern gardens. It often has frosted shoots in spring which need to be cut out.

It is wise to give it winter protection in cold districts. The aromatic leaves are glossy, bright-green, and composed of three leaflets. The flowers are carried in clusters, and are white and scented. This shrub usually has two flushes: April to May, and September to October.

Clematis is a most useful group of hardy twining plants which can be used in a variety of situations: to climb through other shrubs, or up a pergola, arch, tree stump or tripod. Their roots should always be in shade and they like a rich, well-drained, slightly alkaline soil. All except one (Clematis armandii), are deciduous.

They all have opposite leaves, but these vary greatly in size. The flowers are (usually) composed of ovate petal-like sepals. Most of the species have fluffy seedheads.

Basically each plant falls into one of these Pruning Groups:

PG1 Prune after flowering; remove dead or damaged shoots and cut back too-strong growths.

PG2 Prune before new growth starts in late winter. Remove dead and damaged wood and cut back to highest pair of strong buds.

PG3 Prune in early spring down to about 300mm / 1ft from ground.

---

29 *Clematis alpina* **'Frances Rivis'** (PG1) reaches 2 × 1.5m / 6½ × 5ft and will grow on a north aspect the leaf consists of nine dark green, ovate-lanceolate, serrated leaflets. The flowers are pendulous, lantern-shaped, single, blue and 30 × 50mm / 1¼ × 2in wide; they are borne in April and May.

30 *C.* **armandii 'Snowdrift'** (PG1) is the only evergreen clematis and is not reliably hardy. It requires a sheltered south or south-west aspect, and winter protection in cold districts. The leaves are glossy, trifoliate, with lanceolate, veined leaflets. The flowers are white, flat and 50mm / 2in across. They come out in April.

31 *C.* **'Bees Jubilee'** (PG2) likes a north or east aspect. It is not very vigorous, reaching about 2.5m / 8ft. The leaves are trifoliate and the flowers are up to 125mm / 5in wide and single pink with a carmine central stripe on each petal. The flowering season is prolonged: from May until October.

32 *C.* **'Comtesse de Bouchaud'** (PG3) will grow to 3.5m / 11½ft and has soft mauve-pink flowers, with creamy-yellow stamens, up to 140mm / 5½in across, in June and July.

33 *C.* **'Duchess of Albany'** (PG3) reaches 2.5m / 8ft and will do well on any aspect. Its leaves are composed of five leaflets and the flowers are 40 or 50mm / 1½ or 2in long, bright rose-pink and tulip-shaped. It flowers from June to September.

34 *C.* **'Ernest Markham'** (PG3) grows to 2.5m / 8ft, and likes a sunny place. The leaves consist of three or five leaflets. The flowers are 100mm / 4in across, bright red, blunt-tipped, and carried from July until October.

35 *C.* **'Etoile Violette'** is a vigorous cultivar, with vinous purple petals and a creamy centre of stamens, the flower measuring about 100mm / 4in across. Its flowering season is July and August.

36 *C.* **florida 'Sieboldii'** (PG2) is also semi-evergreen. It is not vigorous; it has leaves composed of five leaflets and single, creamy-white flowers with distinctive purple staminodes, in April and May. It likes a westerly aspect.

37 *C.* **'Hagley Hybrid'** (PG3) is also not very vigorous, but it is so useful as it will grow in shade. The flowers are a deep pink with purple anthers about 100mm / 4in across and out between June and September.

38 *C.* **'Huldine'** (PG3) grows up to 3 × 2m / 10 × 6½ft. It is useful for growing up archways or pergolas in almost any aspect, except south. The leaves are composed of five leaflets. The flowers, which come in summer, are single, white (mauve beneath), with cream anthers, 60mm / 2½in across.

39 *C.* **'Jackmanii Superba'** (PG3) grows to a height and spread of 3 × 2m / 10 × 6½ft. The leaves are simple, in threes or fives and the flowers are 75 – 100mm / 3 – 4in across, single, dark vinous-purple. They are borne from July until October. It does best away from strong sunlight, because otherwise the colour may fade.

40 *C.* **'Kermesina'** is a vigorous Viticella hybrid with deep crimson flowers in summer and ternate leaves. Like other Viticellas it will grow in shade.

41 *C.* **macropetala 'Maidwell Hall'** (PG1) likes a north-east or east-facing aspect. The leaf is biternate and the flowers are deep blue open bells with pale blue staminodes. These are borne in May and June.

42 *C.* **'Marie Boisselot'** (syn. **'Mme le Coultre'**) (PG2 or 3) will grow on any aspect. It will grow to about 3m / 10ft. The leaves are simple or in three parts and the flowers are 125mm / 5in wide and consist of overlapping white petals with creamy-white anthers. This clematis flowers between June and the autumn.

43 *C.* **montana** (PG1) is the most widely planted species clematis. It is vigorous, attaining as much as 10m / 33ft in height. The leaf is dark green and trifoliate; the flowers are 50mm / 2in white stars which appears in clusters in early summer. This clematis grows in any position, even deep shade.

44 *C.* **'Nelly Moser'** (PG2) should be given a north, east- or west-facing site and will grow to 3.5m / 11½ft. It has a tripartite leaf and very large (125 – 150mm / 5 – 6in) mauve-pink flowers with a carmine stripe and dark anthers. It begins to flower in May and goes on intermittently until November.

Vertical gardening in the Rose Garden at Sissinghurst, using simple tripods to support *Clematis* 'Ville de Lyon'.

45 *C.* **'Niobe'** (PG2) is a slender, large-flowered hybrid which will grow on any aspect. The flowers, which come between May and September, are 100 – 130mm / 4 – 5in wide, single, and deep red with yellow anthers.

46 *C. tangutica* **'Bill Mackenzie'** (PG3) is immensely vigorous, growing to approximately 7 × 4m / 23 × 13ft. It likes a sunny position. The leaves are grey-green and ferny. The thick petals are up to 50mm / 2in long and look like yellow orange peel; they are out from August until October. These are followed by silvery-green seed heads.

47 *C.* **'Perle d'Azur'** (PG3) is a glorious clematis, memorably associated with the purple-leaved *Vitis vinifera* 'Purpurea' at Sissinghurst. Its abundant flowers are light blue in colour, with four to six petals up to 150mm / 6in wide, from June until August.

48 *C.* **'The President'** (PG2) is a single, large-flowered hybrid, with rich purple petals, which have a silver stripe to them, and red anthers. It will grow up to 3m / 10ft and is suitable for most aspects. It flowers between June and September.

49 *C.* **'Royal Velours'** (PG3) is a Viticella hybrid with rich deep purple flowers, freely borne, but only individually measuring about 35mm / 1¾in across.

50 *C.* **'Vyvyan Pennell'** (PG2) has 100 – 125mm/4-5in wide double (single later) pale mauve flowers between May and November. The leaves are in three parts. It grows to 3.5m / 11½ft and tolerates any aspect.

51 *C.* **'W. E. Gladstone'** (PG2) grows to 3m / 10ft, on any aspect. The large leaves are simple or in three parts and the flowers up to 250mm / 10in, single, lavender in colour, with red anthers. It is a summer-flowerer (June until October).

52 *Clianthus puniceus* is an evergreen, tender,

scrambling shrub, which grows to about 4m / 13ft. It must have a south or west wall, and a well-drained soil. It will, in any case, need winter protection. The leaf is made up of many leaflets; the flowers are drooping 100mm / 4in clusters of claw-like, brilliant red flowers in May and June.

53 *Cobaea scandens* **(cup and saucer)** is a tender annual which does well on a pergola, trellis or wall. It climbs by means of tendrils, to 7.5m / 24½ft or so. It likes a sunny place and well-drained soil. The leaf is composed of three pairs of oval leaflets and the flowers are 60mm / 2¼in long, with a purple bell corolla, green 'saucer' calyx, and protruberant curved stamens. These appear between May and October.

54 *Coronilla glauca* is an evergreen, half-hardy rather lax wall shrub, which grows to 1.2 × 1.2m / 4 × 4ft. It likes a sunny south- or west-facing site, and a light, well-drained soil. It will need winter protection in northern gardens. The leaf is blue-grey, and consists of five to seven leaflets. The flowers are small, yellow, pea-like, and scented. They are evident between April and September, but this shrub is never completely without them in mild weather, even in winter.

55 *Cotoneaster horizontalis* is a common but very useful deciduous wall shrub with a distinctive stiff, herringbone branch habit. It is hardy, and grows to 2 × 1.5m / 6½ × 5ft. It likes any aspect and will grow in any soil. The leaf is glossy, dark green, ovate, and turns red in autumn. The flower is pinkish-white, like miniature apple-blossom, from April until June; the fruit consists of red berries, which the birds enjoy.

56 *Crinodendron hookerianum* is a beautiful and unusual evergreen, half-hardy wall shrub, which likes a moist but well-drained, fertile, acid soil in a shady aspect. It needs winter protection, except in very favoured districts. The leaf is lanceolate, toothed and leathery; the flower waxy, crimson and pendulous, and 25mm / 1in long. These are borne between April and June.

57 *Dendromecon rigida* is an unusual evergreen, tenderish wall shrub, which grows to about 3 × 3m / 10 × 10ft. It needs a south or west wall, a very well-drained soil and winter protection. The leaves are thick, grey-green and lanceolate. The flowers are golden-yellow poppy-like saucers and scented, blooming between April and September.

58 *Desfontainea spinosa* is an evergreen wall shrub, which grows to 1.5 × 1.5m / 5 × 5ft and is happy on any wall except a south-facing one. The soil should be cool, moist and acid. It will need some protection in northern gardens in winter. The leaves are shiny, dark green and spiny; the flowers are 30mm / 1¼in long scarlet, tipped with yellow, pendulous trumpets, out from June until October.

59 *Drimys winteri* **(winter's bark)** is an evergreen, half-hardy wall shrub (or even tree in favoured localities) in time 8 × 3m / 26 × 10ft in height and spread, suitable for south or west walls. It likes a fertile, moist, but well-drained soil, and needs winter protection in cold gardens. The leaves are glossy green, oblong, and glaucous beneath. The May and June flowers are 30mm / 1¼in across, grouped in clusters of seven or eight, white and scented.

60 *Eccremocarpus scaber* is a tender, scrambling annual that can be used to climb through shrubs, up walls and over trellis. It thrives on a south or west aspect, in a well-drained but not impoverished soil. It has pinnate leaves and tendrils and 25mm / 1in long orange-scarlet tubular flowers in racemes, from June until October. They are followed by bladder fruits.

61 *Escallonia* **'Apple Blossom'** is an evergreen hardy wall shrub, 2 × 2.5m / 6½ × 8ft for a south or west wall and a well-drained soil. The leaf is ovate and light green, and the flower cup-shaped, and pale pink. These are borne from June until October.

62 *Escallonia* **'Iveyi'** is also evergreen but only

half-hardy and should have a sunny aspect and a well-drained soil. The leaves are oval and finely toothed, and the flowers (which have recurved petals) are white, 12mm / ½in across, and carried in long terminal panicles in July and August.

63 *Euonymus fortunei* **'Silver Queen'** is a useful hardy, evergreen shrub for a wall or tree stump in sun or partial shade in ordinary soil. It has both juvenile (creeping) and adult (upright) leaf forms and grows in time to about 2 × 2m / 6½ × 6½ft. The leaf is glossy, broad, green with white edges. The flowers are tiny and insignificant – greenish-white in early summer. The fruits are orange seeds in a pink capsule, but not always borne.

64 *Fabiana imbricata violacea* is an evergreen, half-hardy shrub suitable for wall culture, and growing to 2 × 2m / 6½ × 6½ft. It enjoys a sunny aspect and fertile, well-drained soil. It needs winter protection. The leaves are tiny, heath-like, deep green. The flowers are tubular, lilac, 12 – 20mm / ½ – ¾in long, and carried on the ends of branches from May until July.

65 *Forsythia suspensa* looks well against a wall, probably because of its lax growths, which can be tied in easily. It is deciduous, hardy, and will thrive on any aspect or any soil, growing to 3m / 10ft or more. The leaves are ovate, mid-green, and sometimes divided into leaflets; the flowers 25mm / 1in across, bright yellow, pendulous, narrowly trumpet-shaped, and borne in small clusters in March and April.

66 *Fremontodendron* **'California Glory'** is a half-hardy wall shrub which is semi-evergreen in mild winters. It makes a large shrub up to 4 × 2.5m / 13 × 8ft. It likes a south or west wall, and well-drained, sandy soil. It will need some protection in cold districts in winter. The leaves are rounded, lobed and dark green above, with brown hairs below. The flowers, which come out between May and October, are large (up to 65mm / 2¾in), saucer-shaped and bright yellow in colour.

67 *Fuchsia magellanica* **'Versicolor'** is a
deciduous or semi-evergreen shrub, which can be
grown against a wall, where it will reach 1.5 ×
1m / 5 × 3ft. It likes a sunny position and a
free-draining, humus-rich soil. The leaf is prettily
variegated grey-green, with white and pink; the
flowers are 50mm / 2in long, pendant; narrow
crimson tubes with purple petals, and protruding
stamens. These appear all summer and continues
into the autumn.

68 *Garrya elliptica* is an evergreen, dioecious,
almost hardy wall shrub, which will grow to
3 × 2.5m / 10 × 8ft, it grows on any aspect but
flowers best in full sun. It likes a well-drained
soil. The leaves are ovate, leathery, grey-green
and wavy-edged. The panicles of flowers, which
are borne very early in the year, are longest on
male plants 150 – 225mm / 6 – 9in long,
pendulous, and silvery-green. The female plants
will bear purple fruit.

The genus *Hedera* **(the ivies)** are self-
clinging climbers suitable for trellis, wall,
tree stump and pergola. They are
evergreen, usually hardy and will grow on
any aspect and any soil, although they
probably grow best in dryish shade. This
makes them a marvellously useful genus.
There are two types of growth – juvenile
and adult – the first being generally
roughly triangular, and usually lobed, the
second entire. The flowers are yellowish-
green and borne in September and
October. The fruit is usually globose and
black.

---

69 *H. canariensis* **'Gloire de Marengo'** is tenderer
than most ivies; it grows to 5 × 3m / 16½ × 10ft
and prefers a sunny position. It will need winter
protection until established. It has leathery, lobed
leaves, broadly ovate and with a heart-shaped
base; dark green in the middle, they are silver-
grey and white on the margin.

The beauty of the small-leaved, cheerful ivy 'Buttercup', used to clothe an entire wall
at Chartwell, is its self-clinging characteristic, although crumbling walls may suffer
some damage as a result.

70 *H. colchica* **'Dentata Variegata'** is also half-hardy and grows to 5 × 3m / 16½ × 10ft. It also appreciates a sunny aspect and initial winter protection. The leaves are ovate or heart-shaped, 200–250mm / 8–10in long, 150mm / 6in wide, and drooping; they are pale green and yellow.

71 *H. c.* **'Sulphur Heart' (syn. 'Paddy's Pride')** is half-hardy, requiring a warm position and winter protection in the first year in cold districts. The leaves have a yellow central splash, surrounded by pale green.

72 *Hedera helix* **'Atropurpurea'** is hardy, grows to 4 × 2.5m / 13 × 8ft, and is not fussy as to aspect. The leaves are dark green, but turn to purple with green veins in winter.

73 *H. h.* **'Buttercup'** is hardy, grows to 2 × 2.5m / 6½ × 8ft, prefers a south- or west-facing position and has light green leaves which turn yellow in the sun. The leaves are three-lobed.

74 *H. h.* **'Glacier'** is hardy, grows to 3 × 2m / 10 × 6½ft, likes a shady spot and has purple-green stems and silver-grey-green leaves.

75 *H. h.* **'Green Ripple'** is hardy and suitable for a low wall, as it grows to only 1.2 × 1.2m / 4 × 4ft. The deeply-lobed leaves are mid-green with light green veins; they turn coppery in autumn.

76 *H. h.* **'Ivalace'** is hardy, and, at 1 × 1.2m / 3 × 4ft, suitable for a low wall. The leaves are small, dark green and glossy; they are five-lobed and curled at the edges.

77 *Hoheria lyallii* is a deciduous wall tree or shrub, not reliably hardy, which grows up to 4 × 2.5m / 13 × 8ft in time. It will need a south- or south-west-facing position (and winter protection) in cold districts, otherwise it will stand some shade. The soil should be fertile and well-drained. The leaves are deeply toothed, grey-green and downy; clusters of white, saucer-shaped flowers appear in August.

78 *Humulus lupulus aureus* **(golden hop)** is a hardy, twining, herbaceous perennial, suitable for a tree stump, tripod, garage, wall or fence. It is vigorous, growing to 6 × 2m / 19½ × 6½ft. It thrives in any position except deep shade. It likes a well-drained soil. The leaves are toothed and yellow, with three lobes; the female flowers consist of greenish spikes in pendant 20mm / ¾in clusters from July until September. The fruits (hops) are 20mm / 1¾in 'cones'.

79 *Hydrangea aspera villosa* is a reasonably hardy shrub which benefits from wall protection to help save the young shoots being frost damaged in spring. It will grow in shade or semi-shade but is unhappy on an easterly or southerly aspect. It is happiest on a slightly acid soil although it will tolerate lime, and likes rich, deep, damp soils. The leaves are mostly ovate, with a velvety texture, up to 200mm / 8in long, and the flowers are borne in flat heads of both sterile and fertile florets, are pale purple, 150mm / 6in across, in August.

80 *Indigofera heterantha gerardiana* is a half-hardy deciduous shrub, best grown against a wall. It grows to 2 × 1.8m / 6.5 × 6ft and is happiest in a sheltered sunny spot and a well-drained soil. The leaves are grey-green, and pinnate, being composed of 13 to 21 leaflets, and are slow to come in the spring. The flowers appear between July and October, and are 100mm / 4in racemes of purple-pink pea flowers.

81 *Jasminum nudiflorum* **(winter jasmine)** is a deciduous, hardy, scandent climber for wall, fence, trellis, arbour or pergola. It will grow to 3 × 3m / 10 × 10ft. It is not fussy as to aspect, provided it is sheltered from cold winds. Any ordinary, well-drained soil will do. The leaves are oval, dark green and trifoliate. The flowers are bright yellow, 20–30mm / ¾–1¼in long, and borne between November and April.

82 *J. officinale* is suitable for wall, fence, pergola or trellis, being a deciduous, hardy, twining shrub which can grow to 10m / 33ft. It is happiest in a sunny aspect, but any ordinary, well-drained soil will do. The leaves are mid-green, and pinnate, with up to nine leaflets. Pure white (pink in bud), four- or five-lobed, scented flowers appear in small clusters from June to September.

83 *Ipomoea tricolor* **(syn.** *I. rubro-caerulea***) 'Heavenly Blue'** is a tender, twining annual for pergola, wall, trellis or tripod. It grows to approximately 3m / 10ft. It requires a sunny and well-drained site. The leaves are heart-shaped and the large (60mm / 2¼in), sky-blue trumpets come out between July and September, each one lasting only a day.

84 *Lathyrus latifolius* **(everlasting pea)** is a hardy herbaceous perennial, which scrambles using tendrils; it can thus be used for walls, fences, trellis, or to clamber through shrubs. It likes a rich soil, but will stand some shade. The leaves consist of elliptical, glaucous-green leaflets, and the stems are winged. The flowers are rose-purple, and borne in many-flowered peduncles, 250–300mm / 10–12in long, from June until September.

Lonicera **(honeysuckle)** is a genus suitable for wall, fence, arch or pergola. Some species are deciduous, others evergreen. All mentioned are hardy twining shrubs, which like an ordinary, well-drained soil, to which organic matter has been added. They also like their roots to be in shade but their heads in the sun. The flowers are often scented, borne in clusters, and tubular with two distinct lips in shape.

85 *L.* × *brownii* is semi-evergreen, growing up to 3m / 10ft. The leaves are oval, mid-green above, and glaucous below. The flowers are borne in terminal whorls, and are slender, scarlet, 25–50mm / 1–2in long, but unscented. They appear between June and September and are sometimes followed by red berries.

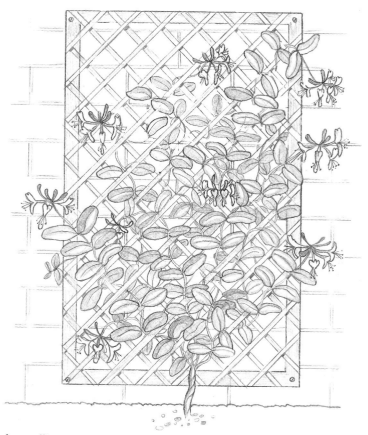

Wooden trellis against a wall is a suitable alternative to wires as the support for twining climbers, such as *Lonicera × americana*, provided the trellis is nailed to battens to leave a gap between trellis and wall.

86 *L. periclymenum* 'Serotina' (late Dutch honeysuckle) is deciduous, and grows to about 5m / 16½ft. The leaf is ovate. The flowers, which appear between July and October, are borne in terminal whorls; they are red-purple on the outside, creamy-white inside, and scented. Bright red berries follow.

87 *L. × tellmanniana* is deciduous and, although hardy, likes a sunny position, where it will grow to about 5m / 16½ft. The stalkless leaves are grey-green and ovate; the whorls of yellow-orange, 50mm / 2in big, flowers in summer.

88 *Magnolia grandiflora* is a very large, evergreen, slightly tender, wall tree or shrub, which can easily grow to 5m / 16½ft or more in time, with a similar spread. Ideally, it should be planted facing south or west to encourage good flowering. It likes a well-drained loam and will benefit from initial winter protection. The leaves are very big (up to 250mm / 10in long) glossy, ovate and leathery, with a thick down of rust-coloured hairs on the undersides. The flowers are cream-white, thick-petalled, heavily lemon-scented and bowl-shaped, about 100 – 200mm / 4 – 8in across. They are mainly borne between

July and September, although the odd flower appears at other times.

89 *Myrtus communis* (common myrtle) is an evergreen, tender wall shrub, which must have winter protection in all but favoured districts. It grows to about 2.5 × 2.5m / 8 × 8ft. It requires a sunny position, but will grow in an ordinary soil, if well-drained. The leaves are glossy, deep green, and round or ovate in shape. The flowers are 25mm / 1in wide, white, with protruding stamens and appear in summer, followed by purple-black ovoid berries.

90 *Passiflora caerulea* (passion flower) is a slightly tender evergreen or semi-evergreen, scandent shrub, suitable for trellis, arbour or wall. It clings by means of tendrils, and needs wire mesh or trellis for support. It can reach 6m / 19½ft in a sunny place and an ordinary, well-drained soil. The leaves are palmate, with five- or seven-lobed leaflets, and mid green. The fragrant flowers, carried from June until September, are most unusual, having white, flushed pink, sepals and petals with blue or purple filaments. The fruits are ovoid and yellow but only produced after hot summers. The leaves turn yellow in autumn.

91 *Pileostegia viburnoides* is an evergreen half-hardy, self-clinging shrub. Its spread is 5 × 3m / 16½ × 10ft. It is suitable for arch, pergola or rough-barked tree trunk, and will grow in any aspect or any well-drained soil. It needs winter protection in cold districts. The leaves are ovate, lanceolate, and leathery with prominent veins; the flowers are tiny, white or cream, with many prominent stamens, in panicles, up to 150mm / 6in long. They appear between July and September.

92 *Piptanthus nepalensis* is a semi-evergreen, half-hardy, wall shrub, which grows to 2.5 × 2m / 8 × 6½ft. It likes a south- or west-facing situation and, if possible, a well-drained, sandy loam. It is best protected in cold gardens in winter. The leaves are lanceolate, dark green (with silver hairs when young), and cut into three leaflets. The flowers are like bright yellow scented pea flowers, in 50 – 100mm / 2 – 4in long racemes. They flower in late spring.

93 *Pittosporum tenuifolium* is a half-hardy shrub which does well in mild coastal areas, but benefits from a wall elsewhere. It grows to more than 3 × 1.5m / 10 × 5ft in time. The grey-green leaves are oval, 30 – 60mm / 1 – 2½in long, thick, glossy with wavy margins; the stems are black. The flowers are scented, chocolate-purple in colour, small and borne in late spring, but only on mature plants.

94 *Prunus triloba* **'Multiplex'** is a deciduous, hardy, wall shrub, which can attain 3m / 10ft by as much across. It is happiest on a sunny aspect and in a well-drained soil. The leaves are bright green, oval, and often three-lobed; they turn yellow before they fall. The flowers are double, clear pink, and rosette-shaped, up to 25mm / 1in across and carried in March and April.

95 *Pyracantha* **'Mohave'** is an evergreen wall-shrub, which is not quite so hardy as other pyracanthas. It grows to 2.5 × 3m / 8 × 10ft on a, preferably, semi-shaded wall. It likes a fertile, well-drained soil. The leaves are mid-green, and oblanceolate in shape; the flowers are small and white, and carried in clusters in June. The berries are prolific, orange-red, and to be seen from mid-August onwards.

96 *P. coccinea* **'Lalandei'** is a hardy, evergreen, wall shrub which can reach 5m / 16½ft in time. It is happy in full or partial shade and in any soil except heavy clay. The leaf is oval and the flowers white, 8mm / ⅓in across, borne in clusters in June. The fruits are orange-red.

97 *P.* **'Watereri'** is similar but is suitable for a shorter wall because it grows to about 2.5m / 8ft. The leaves are elliptic, the flowers white, borne in clusters in June, and the berries deep orange-red.

98 *Ribes speciosum,* a relation of the gooseberry, is a deciduous, slightly tender wall shrub, which grows to 2 × 1.5m / 6.5 × 5ft. It is best on a sunny aspect and ordinary but well-drained soil. This plant has densely and unpleasantly spined stems, and deeply lobed, mid-green leaves. The flowers are fuchsia-like – bright red, 25 – 30mm / 1 – 1¼in long, in clusters in late spring and early summer.

99 *Rhodochiton atrosanguineus*/(syn. *R. volubilis*) is a tender annual twining climber. It grows to about 3m / 10ft. It should be grown in a well-drained soil and sunny place. The leaves are heart-shaped and have marginal teeth. The flowers are pendulous and produced singly. They consist of a five-lobed calyx, which is bell-shaped, 25mm / 1in long, and reddish-purple, and a blackish-purple corolla, 50mm / 2in long, which divides into five rounded lobes at the end. These flowers are produced in summer.

100 *Robinia hispida* is a deciduous, hardy, wall shrub, which grows to 3 × 3m / 10 × 10ft, and can be fan-trained. It requires a sheltered and sunny aspect, and a well-drained, even dry soil. The leaves are pinnate, acacia-like, on bristly stems, and the attractive rose-pink pea flowers, 25 – 30mm / 1 – 1¼in long, are borne in drooping racemes in May and June.

Rosa are deciduous, mainly hardy, scrambling shrubs which, according to type, will furnish walls, pillars, pergolas, arches or tree stumps. Most like an open sunny position, although some climbers do well in trees, while others will thrive on a north wall provided there is plenty of light. Roses like good drainage, a soil pH of about 6.5, which is humus rich; they are not so happy on sandy, chalky or clayey soils. The leaves vary but are predominantly oval and consisting of several leaflets. Roses are often scented and usually flower in June, and often all summer (depending on variety) or with a second flush in September.

101 *R.* **'Albéric Barbier'** is a once-flowering vigorous rambler that is useful for arch, pergola or trellis, and has distinctive glossy green leaves and flowers, yellow in bud, opening into large white and pale lemon clusters.

102 *R.* **'Albertine'** is a beautiful once-flowering vigorous rambler that can be used as a weeping standard, or for growing up an arch or pergola; it is best not against a wall because it is prone to mildew. The fragrant flowers are double, and a glowing copper pink, which hang on after they have faded.

103 *R.* **'Allen Chandler'** grows to 5m / 16½ft and is suitable for a large house wall. The 100mm / 4in wide flowers are recurrent, semi-double, and vivid dark red with golden stamens.

104 *R.* **'Bobbie James'** grows up to 8m / 26ft so can be planted to climb a tree. It has creamy-white, single or semi-double, scented flowers in large trusses in June and July.

105 *R.* **'Compassion'** is another pillar rose, with large, double, apricot-copper, scented flowers that are repeated. It has dark green, glossy leaves.

106 *R.* **'Constance Spry'** grows to 3m / 10ft or more, and makes a splendid scented display with its large, 100mm / 4in wide, soft pink, old-fashioned flowers in June and July.

107 *R.* **'Debutante'** is an old rambler, dating from 1902, which flowers once but very freely, with scented rose-pink flowers borne in clusters. It can be used for climbing through old fruit trees, and is disease resistant.

108 *R.* **'François Juranville'** is a popular and vigorous, 7m / 23ft, rambler with coral-pink, double, fragrant, large flowers, which does well on pergola or trellis.

109 *R.* **'Goldfinch'** is another rambler, which is less vigorous and robust and likes to be sheltered

A stunning display of 'Constance Spry' roses
at Mottisfont.

from cold winds. The flowers are large, scented, golden-yellow fading to light yellow, and come early and in profusion.

110 *R.* **'Leverkusen'** is a pillar or wall rose with pale yellow, semi-double scented blooms that flower in sprays on long stems in June and then again in September.

111 *R.* **'Madame Alfred Carrière'** grows to 3m / 10ft and has blush-pink, slightly untidy blooms in June and recurrently through the summer. It will grow in sun or shade and is suitable for walls or for growing up through a tree.

112 *R.* **'New Dawn'** is suitable for a tree stump or pillar, usually growing to around 2.5 × 2.5m / 8 × 8ft. The flowers are silver pink, double, and smell of apples and appear almost continuously until September.

113 *R.* **'Paul's Scarlet Climber'** is a not very vigorous rose suitable for a pillar or trellis. It will also grow on any aspect. The flowers are scarlet, semi-double, and carried in clusters from June until September.

114 *R.* **'Pompon de Paris', Climbing** is a non-vigorous miniature climbing rose, usually only reaching 2m/6½ft; it is thus suitable to grow through a shrub such as a ceanothus. It likes a sheltered position. The flowers, which do not recur, are very small, pink and double.

115 *Schizophragma integrifolium* is a deciduous, hardy, self-clinging shrub for a tall wall, pergola, or tree trunk. It grows up to 7m / 23ft or more in time. It likes a semi-shaded or sunny site in a rich, moisture-retentive, humus-rich soil. The leaves are ovate, bright green above and grey-green beneath. The flat inflorescences, up to 300mm / 12in across, consist of small, white flowers surrounded by 80mm / 3in long white sepals. These appear between July and September.

116 *Solanum crispum* **'Glasnevin'** is a vigorous, semi-evergreen, scandent plant for a wall, fence, or even a garage roof. More or less hardy, it nevertheless does best in a sunny place. It is not fussy as to soil. The leaves are dark green and ovate. The clusters of bluish-purple potato flowers with the characteristic yellow cone of anthers, each 25mm / 1in wide, are carried from June until September.

117 *S. jasminoides* **'Album'** is evergreen, half-hardy and twining. It grows to 6m / 19½ft or so and requires a sunny site and winter protection. The leaves are ovate and sometimes divided into leaflets; the flowers, which come out between July and October, are white with yellow anthers, and very showy.

118 *Trachelospermum jasminoides* is evergreen, half-hardy, twining and self-clinging, and suitable for wall or fence. It likes a sheltered and sunny aspect and a light, well-drained, but not droughty, acid soil. The leaves are dark green, leathery, and elliptic or ovate-lanceolate; the flowers are white, with recurved petals, scented, 25mm / 1in across, and held in slender clusters at the ends of shoots in July and August.

119 *Tropaeolum peregrinum* **(canary creeper)** is a half-hardy annual for a wall, fence or tree. it is a scrambler and grows to about 3m / 10ft. It prefers a sunny position but is not fussy as to soil. The leaves are grey-green with five broad lobes. The flowers are somewhat irregular in shape and consist of three bright yellow petals, with two upper petals that are larger and fringed. These come out between July and October.

120 *T. speciosum* **(flame creeper)** is deciduous, hardy, perennial, and climbs by twining and has a creeping rootstock. It will grow through hedges or shrubs, or against a wall. It likes its roots in shade but its head in the sun. The soil should be moisture-retentive, acid or neutral with peat added. The leaves are mid-green and six-lobed. The flowers are brilliant scarlet, 30mm / 1¼in across, and consist of five rounded and notched petals. These are produced between July and September.

121 *Vitis vinifera* **'Purpurea' (teinturier grape)** is a deciduous, hardy, scrambling vine which grows to about 6m / 19½ft, making it suitable for growing up a tree or wall. It prefers a sunny aspect, if possible. The leaves are round, lobed and claret-red, and white-haired when young, which lends them a grey-purple patina. The flowers in June are tiny; inedible, oval, purple-black grapes follow. The autumn leaf colour is a rich dark purple-red.

122 *Wisteria sinensis* **'Alba'** is a deciduous, hardy and twining plant, known to grow to 30m / 98½ft and which has no difficulty reaching 10m / 33ft. It likes to be in a sunny position, where the flower buds are protected from cold winds and frost in spring. It should be put in moisture-retentive, fertile soil if possible. The leaf consists of 11 leaflets and the late spring flowers are white, highly scented, and in dense and elegant racemes 200 – 300mm / 8 – 12in long. There is often some flower in late summer.

NATIONAL TRUST GARDENS

Below are the addresses and telephone numbers of National Trust Gardens particularly noted for climbers and wall plants

Acorn Bank, *Temple Sowerby, near Penrith, Cumbria (07683) 61893*

Barrington Court, *nr Ilminster, Somerset (0460) 40601/52242*

Blickling Hall, *Norwich, Norfolk (0263) 733084*

Bodnant, *Tal-y-Cafn, Colwyn Bay, Clwyd (0492) 650460 (during office hours)*

Coleton Fishacre, *Coleton, Kingswear, Dartmouth, Devon (080425) 466*

Erddig, *nr Wrexham, Clywd (0978) 355314 (during office hours)*

Felbrigg Hall, *Norwich, Norfolk (0263) 75444*

Gunby Hall, *Gunby, nr Spilsby, Lincolnshire (for opening hours call National Trust regional office (0909) 486411)*

Hidcote Manor Garden, *Hidcote Bartrim, nr Chipping Camden, Gloucestershire (0386) 438 333*

Knightshayes Court, *Bolham, Tiverton, Devon (0884) 254665*

Lanhydrock, *Bodmin, Cornwall (0208) 73320*

Mottisfont Abbey, *Mottisfont, nr Romsey, Hampshire (0794) 41220/40757*

Mount Stewart, *Newtownards, Co. Down, Northern Ireland (024 774) 387*

Peckover House, *North Brink, Wisbech, Cambridgeshire (0945) 583463*

Penrhyn Castle, *Bangor, Gwynedd, Wales (0248) 353084*

Polesden Lacey, *nr Dorking, Surrey (0372) 458203/452048*

Powis Castle, *Welshpool, Powys (0938) 554336*

Rowallane Garden, *Saintfield, Ballynahinch, County Down, Northern Ireland (0238) 510131*

Sissinghurst Castle, *Sissinghurst, nr Cranbrook, Kent (0580) 712850*

Tintinhull, *Tintinhull, nr Yeovil, Somerset (for opening times call NT regional office (0474) 840224)*

Upton House, *Banbury, Oxfordshire (029 587) 266*

Wakehurst Place Garden, *Ardingly, nr Haywards Heath, West Sussex (0444) 892701*

Wallington, *Cambo, Morpeth, Northumberland (067 074) 283*

GLOSSARY OF TERMS

Adventitious: refers to roots which do not arise from the plant's original root, such as aerial roots.

Aerial root: root which arises from stems which are above ground, such as those on *Hedera* or *Hydrangea anomala petiolaris*.

Axil: the angle between stem and leaf.

Bipinnate: refers to a leaf which is divided into segments which are themselves divided.

Biternate: leaf which is divided and sub-divided into threes.

Bract: modified leaf.

Bud: immature leaves, and/or flowers. Also marking on stem from which side shoots will come.

Compost: either a growing medium for seeds, cuttings and small plants or a well-rotted mixture of vegetable waste, lawn clippings, annual weeds and soil; the result is often called humus (see below).

Corymb: flat-topped cluster of flowers, such as cow parsley flowers.

Dioecious: refers to plants which bear male and female parts on different plants.

Globose: spherical.

Humus: either well-rotted garden compost or black colloidal material in the soil made of completely decayed vegetable matter.

Hybrid: plant which is the result of a cross between two distinct species, sub-species, varieties or, very occasionally, genera.

Inflorescence: grouping of flowers on a plant.

Lanceolate: leaf-shape which is broadest at the base.

Lateral: side-shoot.

Linear: narrow leaf with parallel sides.

Mulch: layer of organic or polythene material laid on the ground to discourage weeds and/or conserve moisture.

Node: joint on a stem from whence side shoots or leaves arise.

Oblanceolate: reverse of lanceolate, ie leaf which tapers to its base.

Obovate: broad leaf which tapers somewhat towards base.

Ovate: oval leaf-shape.

Palmate: leaf the shape of a hand with five fingers.

Panicle: branched inflorescence with many stalked flowers such as lilac.

Peduncle: stem that supports a flower head.

Pinnate: leaf which is divided into several pairs of leaflets..

Raceme: unbranched inflorescence made up of stalked flowers, such as wisteria.

Recurved: curving back petals and leaves.

Remontant: plants, which flower more than once in the season, such as roses.

Rootstock: propagation term for a plant onto which another is grafted.

Sport: part of a plant that arises spontaneously, usually either a shoot or flower of a different colour; these can be propagated vegetatively – that is, by cuttings or grafting, as distinct from propagation by seed.

Trifoliate: leaf divided into three.

Tripartite: petal, leaf, sepal or bract which is divided into three.

Variegated: usually leaves which are marked or spotted with another colour or colours.

SELECTED BIBLIOGRAPHY

Bean, W. J. *Trees and Shrubs Hardy in the British
Isles Vols 1 – 4* and *Supplement,*
John Murray, 1976 – 88.

Boisset, Caroline. *Vertical Gardening,*
Mitchell Beazley, 1988.

Davis, Brian. *The Gardener's Illustrated
Encyclopaedia of Climbers and Wall Shrubs,*
Viking 1990.

Grey-Wilson, C. and Matthews, V. *Gardening on
Walls,* Collins, 1983.

Lloyd, C. and Bennett, T. M. *Clematis,* Viking, 1989.

Philip, C. and Lord, A. *The Plant Finder,*
Headmain Ltd (for The Hardy Plant Society), 1991.

Preston, George. *Climbing and Wall Plants,*
Wisley Handbook Series, Cassell, 1986.

Saville, Diana. *Walled Gardens,* Batsford, 1982.

Thomas, G. S. *Climbing Roses Old and New,*
Dent, 1978.

INDEX

ACKNOWLEDGEMENTS

First and foremost, I should like to acknowledge their assistance and thank the head gardeners of National Trust properties who have been so generous with their time and so patient in answering questions; it has been a pleasure and an education to tap such a deep reservoir of knowledge and experience. I am grateful also to the many Public Affairs Managers of the National Trust who have been helpful in providing me with information. I owe a debt of thanks to Penelope Hobhouse, editor of this series, who kindly asked me to write the book and to Margaret Willes and Tony Lord for looking over and correcting the typescript. Any mistakes that remain are my own. Lastly, I should like to thank the team at Pavilion, in particular Louise Simpson and Emily Wright.

Ursula Buchan, 1991

The publishers wish to thank the National Trust and its photographers for their kind permission to reproduce the following photographs:
John Bethell: p. 55; **Neil Campbell-Sharp:** pp. 13, 41, 58, 78, 103; **Vera Collingwood:** p. 51; **Eric Crichton:** pp. 9, 12, 16, 27, 29, 30/31, 54, 56, 95, 97; **Will Curwen:** p. 85; **Jerry Harpur:** p. 67; **E.M. Kirk:** p. 39; **Rob Matheson:** pp. 6, 21, 47; **Nick Meers:** pp. 11, 37; **National Trust Photographic Library:** p. 22/3; **Ian Shaw:** pp. 24, 36, 49, 68, 89, 99; **Richard Surman:** pp. 34/5, 50; **Robert Thrift:** p. 26; **Mike Warren:** p. 86/7; **Mike Williams:** pp. 45, 48.
The publishers also wish to thank the following for their kind permission to reproduce the following photographs:
Tony Lord: pp. 8, 32, 33, 46; **Hugh Palmer:** pp. 2, 15, 20, 25, 33, 38.